To: Mary
The best O.

Helen

M000284028

Fluffy, Funny, and Fabulous

Fluffy, Funny, and Fabulous

A Tale of Five Sisters

Anita Lewis, Vicki Foley, Linda Tarmichael,
Ruth Kenyon, and Helen Landrum

TATE PUBLISHING
AND ENTERPRISES, LLC

Fluffy, Funny, and Fabulous
Copyright © 2012 by Anita Lewis, Vicki Foley, Linda Tarmichael,
Ruth Kenyon, and Helen Landrum. All rights reserved.

No part of this publication may be reproduced, stored in a retrieval system or transmitted in any way by any means, electronic, mechanical, photocopy, recording or otherwise without the prior permission of the author except as provided by USA copyright law.

Scripture quotations marked "NIV" are taken from the *Holy Bible, New International Version* ®, Copyright © 1973, 1978, 1984 by International Bible Society. Used by permission of Zondervan Publishing House. All rights reserved.

The opinions expressed by the author are not necessarily those of Tate Publishing, LLC.

Published by Tate Publishing & Enterprises, LLC
127 E. Trade Center Terrace | Mustang, Oklahoma 73064 USA
1.888.361.9473 | www.tatepublishing.com

Tate Publishing is committed to excellence in the publishing industry. The company reflects the philosophy established by the founders, based on Psalm 68:11,
"The Lord gave the word and great was the company of those who published it."

Book design copyright © 2012 by Tate Publishing, LLC. All rights reserved.
Cover design by Jomel Pepito
Interior design by Rodrigo Adolfo

Published in the United States of America

ISBN: 978-1-62147-464-7
1. Family & Relationships / Siblings
2. Biography & Autobiography / Personal Memoirs
12.09.26

Table of Contents

Family 1977

Family Photo 1963

Chris Walk

Dad and Max

Aunt Mary and Uncle Bill

Cat House

Grandma and Grandpa Schmitt

Mom and Dad

Mom and Dad's Wedding

Mom at Plum Landing

Mom with tapestry

Mom

Sexy sisters

Sisters at Jelly Belly Factory

Sisters with Elvis Impersonator

Vicki, Ruth, Anita, Helen, and Linda
in Spring of 1959

Vicki

Linda

Sisters and brother-in-law John during Cabo trip

Helen and Ruth

Foreword

*H*aving spent time with all five sisters, I determined in my heart that I was going to become one of them also. My wife, Ruth, laughed at the idea. With much determination, I went to her sisters and said, "I love you all so much. Would you consider me to be a sister with all of you? If I remember correctly, their response was overwhelming! I don't remember exactly what Helen said. I believe that Anita agreed to take me in!

Regardless of the outcome, I will always consider myself as part of the sisterhood. I have been blessed to have spent many years and to have had many adventures with them. They really are a part of me.

I thank them all for the kindness they have shown me.

—John Kenyon

Preface

When the five of us get together, we always come back to our memories of growing up. Our ages span nearly twenty years, so our memories are oftentimes very different. This creates some interesting dialogue. One sister starts out a story, and the others soon chime in with their version. Whenever we are all together, we get comments from others saying they wish they were a sister. We hope this book offers some humor, memories, and even a little reflection.

Sincerely,
The Sisters

Growing Up in a Small Town

Anita

*V*irgil, Illinois, was, and for the most part still is, a small farming community of about 200 German Catholics all related to each other somehow. Two main streets in town—IC Trail Road, traveling east and west, and Meredith Road, which was a north/south route—intersected at the general store, and the town was divided in half by the railroad and Route 64, which carried you to the larger towns of St. Charles or Sycamore.

Fritz's General Store was the hub of the town. Town dwellers had to go the store to get their mail. The folks who did not live in town got their mail via the rural route postal carrier, but everyone gathered at the store for supplies and their daily dose of gossip. We kids loved the store because we were able to get ice cold drinks in glass bottles, my favorite being orange soda. Weekly, after we got our allowance, we would pay our nickel, open the bottle with the opener nailed on the wall, and rush outside to sit on the front stoop and then slowly savor every last drop of the cool liquid. When we finished, we would take the empty bottles back inside and place them gently in the wooden storage container to be picked up later by the Pop Man. We then spent whatever few cents we had left on the penny candy invitingly displayed beneath a huge glass case positioned near the store register. When we had finally reached that all-important decision, we would tap our coins on the glass to get the attention of the storekeeper. Half deaf, Fritz was a cantankerous old man who was always annoyed at the amount of time we took to select our sweets, and he was even more annoyed when we demanded his attention with our tapping.

The townspeople, except for two Protestant families, attended St. Peter and Paul Catholic Church, and the children got their elementary education at the attached school. The original school was attended by both our parents. Dad went through sixth grade before leaving to tend to the family farm, and Mom graduated with her eighth-grade diploma. All five of us girls attended the school, taught by the Franciscan nuns, until we had to transfer to the public high school for secondary education.

Most of my memories in Virgil are about growing up with Linda and Vicki. Helen and Ruth are older, and both left the house soon after I was born, so they were never part of my day-to-day childhood. I always thought of them more as Mom's friends than my sisters.

No organized activities existed in Virgil, so all the local kids passed the time away with outdoor games. Our neighbor's house was once upon a time the schoolhouse.

Swings still occupied the west side of the property, and a large grassy area between our house and theirs served as the gathering place for all activities. As soon as school let out, everybody ran home and changed out of their school attire, and a rousing baseball game ensued. When nightfall hit, our baseball game changed to Twelve O'clock the Ghost Comes Out or Kick the Can. This pattern stayed with us all year, even throughout the summer months, except in snowy months, when flag football replaced baseball.

Mom stayed at home and took care of the family. Looking back, I have come to realize what an extraordinary job she did, but at the time it was my father who I adored. Dad worked for the Modern Dairy Milk Company. I never had any idea what his job entailed, but I am sure to this day he had a position of importance.

Originally, the dairy was located in town, across from the general store, but sometime over the years, it was relocated to Elgin. Instead of walking a short block to work, Dad had to make a fifty-mile round-trip drive daily. His schedule was as regular as the Elgin Watch he kept in his pocket. He left every morning as the sun rose, and he returned every eve before dark to the smell of a hot meal on the table. Dad loved to bring little things home from work. If a toy or trinket found its way into one of the glass milk bottles that came into the plant, it ended up in Dad's pocket for distribution to one of us after supper.

On one warm summer's evening, Dad returned from work with a special surprise loaded in the back of his red pickup. It was a big crate, measuring at least six feet by three feet by three feet high. He explained to us that he was going to make a cathouse for us. We always had a bunch of cats running around outside our house. It was not uncommon to have five to ten felines in our yard on any given day.

Dad was always creating something with his hands—a remnant of his days on the family farm—so we were all excited to see how this project might turn out. He painted the crate white; made a roof for it, complete with green shingles; and added a small window on the side and a front door, of course. The roof was removable so the inside of the house could be cleaned. He then placed the house on a slab of concrete located on the far side of our driveway near the other neighbor's house.

Our cats were so impressed by their new mansion— they must have invited every other cat in the neighborhood over to party. Soon our driveway had become the gathering place of the locals, and their owners always knew where to find them when they disappeared. Dad loved the appreciative animals and was always the gracious host, offering milk and food to all.

On the rare occasion when no community games were in process, my sisters Linda and Vicki invented activities to keep us entertained. One of the favorites became the Cat Club, inspired by Dad's creation and our love of cats. The three of us created a clubhouse, complete with a large slate chalkboard in the back room of the basement.

The Cat Club had very strict and solemn rules etched on the slate board, overseen by Her Majesty, the Queen of the Cats. The rules included such things as who had to take the queen's turn washing dishes that night. After all, royalty could not get their hands wet. Another rule was that the queen always got her pick of any litter of kittens born. These were very important things to us, so being elected queen was a great honor. All three of us had an equal vote in who ruled as the queen, but no vote should be cast for one's self.

I am the youngest of the girls, but my dear sisters viewed me as being spoiled; this resulted in them always picking on me, particularly Linda. I was no match for her because I was chubby and not very agile. Linda's favorite torture was to get me down on the ground and wave her long, thick auburn hair back and forth across my face until I started to weep uncontrollably or cry "uncle." Vicki had asthma and also a bad temper, if provoked. Mean Linda Jean took advantage of that weakness by pestering her until Vicki became so enraged that she would fight back. Linda was a good athlete, so she would take off running down the stairs, outside, or even down the streets until Vicki, tired, was forced to stop because she couldn't breathe.

One time Linda decided it would be fun to provoke both Vicki and me by pretending she had a mouse in a trap. She called us outside, and as we screamed at the sight of the trap, she chased us all the way through the backyards of several neighbors to the general store. Finally, we reached the safety of the store, panting and sick, realizing that under no circumstances would Linda be carrying a mouse.

At the end of the voting for Queen of the Cats, Vicki was always elected by a vote of two to one. Linda and I both voted for her, and she took turns voting for either

Linda or me, depending on who she most favored on that day.

All hail the Great Victoria, Queen of the Cats.

Vicki

Growing up in Virgil was quite different than in the bigger towns, like Maple Park and Elburn, which both boasted populations of over 500. We entertained ourselves by playing outside and riding bikes. I had an older bike that was handed down to me from my older sisters. It was an old, ugly blue Schwinn. Being an artistic person, I painted it orange and black tiger-striped and purchased tiger heads for the handlebars. As I pedaled down the blacktop road on my tiger, I thought we were both really cool. We always felt safe riding around town, except when we rode past a couple of farms that had dogs. They would bark and chase us; we had to peddle so fast! Also, there was "Wild Cat Woods." Local legend told of a wild cat being in these woods, so we had to be on high alert when riding past this stretch of road. We never laid eyes on the predator, probably due to the fact that we rode by so fast or maybe out of fear of my tiger bike, which caused it to retreat into the heavy brush of the woods.

On hot summer nights, we'd take a glass jar with nail holes pounded into the lid and head to the vacant lot next door to catch lightning bugs. For some unknown reason, Mom, who hated bugs of any type, would let us keep these little guys with the blinking tails in our room overnight to be released in the morning.

Nita told you about all our cats, but she didn't mention the chickens. Dad bought us three chickens—Pinky, Willie, and Tiny. Willie was incredibly mean—and no, he was not Linda's chicken. I know you thought he would be, but he actually belonged to Nita. We were cautious as we stepped out of the house because Willy might be waiting to peck at your heels. The best thing to do was to run really fast until we reached the merry-go-round, and we would get it spinning so fast that he never caught us.

You might think we all turned out to be runners, as we were always running from something. That brings me to the time I ran away from home. My parents had a feud going with our next-door neighbors. I still don't know what about, but their daughter, Debbie—my best friend—and I were forbidden to play together. Since we were only seven years old, we were both disturbed by our parents' actions and felt we needed to do something to restore the peace. One of my sisters, Ruth, told me that we should run away and then our parents would have to talk to each other and get together to try to find us. So we did. We both packed a suitcase and headed down the road to the Catholic Church. I don't even know what we might have packed in those suitcases, and I don't remember much more about the incident because I think we got into a lot of trouble and I have erased that from my mind. You can't always listen to what your sisters tell you.

Not a lot of exciting events took place in the sleepy little town of Virgil. Summer days were particularly long and quiet. My sisters and I spent endless hours outdoors, and every small detail of the town became permanently part of us. Roads were usually quiet, so when visitors arrived, it was big news.

One of these visitors was the gas deliveryman. Every kid knew his schedule and waited anxiously at the end of their driveway in anticipation of his arrival and the Tootsie Rolls he would bring as a treat for us. (FYI, I remember gas being .34 a gallon.) Another exciting thing was when the Schwan man or the Charles Chip man came. The Schwan man had a refrigerated delivery truck in which he carried all sorts of delectable ice cream treats to be purchased by Mom and put in our standup freezer on the porch. The Charles Chip man delivered all sorts of potato chips and cookies in big metal tins that could be reused to package homemade cookies or any other things that Mom needed to put in storage. It was no wonder that I was overweight as a child with all of these things coming right to our doorstep.

A creek (pronounced *crick*) was located on the edge of town past several farmers' cornfields. We liked to ride our bikes or walk down there. We came up with some great adventures and even went through the tunnel running under the railroad tracks. Some others had also been there before us, as we found writing on the walls.

Cool rocks and wildflowers along the bank of the creek made a great area for a picnic. I think now about these carefree times when we would be gone for hours. Our parents were never concerned because these were safer times. Virgil was a safe, sleepy town full of good people and good memories.

Linda

Growing up in Virgil felt like living in your own little sheltered world. We were not a wealthy family, but we kids never knew it. For example, my swimming pool consisted of an old washtub, but what fun I had in it. When it rained, we were allowed to go out and play in the rain as long as it wasn't thundering or lightning. We would place sticks in the culvert out in front of our house so that when it rained, it would fill with water, and then we would swim in it.

Living in the country caused us to be pretty tough little kids. I can remember learning to ride a bike. My dad would just give me a push and tell me to keep on pedaling. I hit a tree a couple of times and returned home with lots of skinned knees, but I learned how to ride that bike. This was a skill I put to good use since it was my only mode of transportation for sixteen years!

Baseball was another activity we used to play every day during the summer in our neighbor's side yard. I was good at it, and I could keep up with the boys due to my speed and playing ability.

Winter sports consisted of sledding at the factory hill and ice skating at the creek or skating on a pond that formed in the field behind our house. I loved winter and would spend hours trying to perfect my skating routine.

Peggy Fleming was my idol! Of course, these activities were only allowed after helping dad shovel the driveway. Vicki was pretty sickly, so she couldn't help with those tasks, and Nita was too young.

Every Monday was laundry day. Mom would haul baskets of laundry down to our basement and put it in our wringer washer. After the wash cycle finished, we helped her thread the wet garments through the wringer and guided them into the laundry basket. She would then haul the clothes up the stairs and outside to the backyard, where the clothesline, strung between two large poles, was located. We would then take the clothespins out of the clothespin bag and secure the sheets and other clothing on the line to dry.

Before Dad worked at the Modern Dairy in Elgin, he worked at Western United Dairy, which was right across the street. That dairy used to be a factory, and the old property served as an amazing place for outdoor adventures. A large hill along the back side of the property became the local sledding resort in winter. Several other areas were covered with prairie grass and other wildflowers blooming every spring and summer. The neighbor kids and I used to go over and pretend we were the kids from the book *The Boxcar Children.* People used to dump their trash on the site, so we would find all kinds of treasures to use for our survival: old tobacco tins, pieces of broken dishes, and old lumber to make a three-legged chair or table. Our imaginations ran rampant.

We loved animals! Fortunately for us, Dad shared that passion. Mom tolerated pets as long as they didn't live in the house. We had about fifteen cats. We had Carrot, Kohlrabi, and my cat, Turnip. I used to tell Turnip all of my secrets and discuss everything with her. It was a good thing dad worked at the Modern Dairy Company, because he was allowed to bring the expired milk products home for our cats. Our cats feasted regularly on cottage cheese, whole milk, buttermilk, and even chocolate milk! We had rabbits for a while, but I yearned for a pet skunk like my Uncle Willie raised. Mom would have none of that.

As far as me being mean, I don't know what my sisters are talking about! I may have been a little bossy, but since Mom was so busy with the housework, she didn't have time to discipline Vicki and Nita, so I tried to help her. I think Vicki and Nita should be thanking me because without my discipline, they might not have turned out to be such outstanding sisters!

Ruth

My childhood toys did not come from Little Tikes or Fisher Price. The Sears Wish Book came every fall, and it was just that, a wish book. I never actually received any of those items, like an Easy Bake Oven, but looking at those glossy-colored photos got my imagination working. I would spend hours making up concoctions in my secret bakery, located in our backyard, hidden away behind the garage. I envisioned myself a master chef working with key ingredients of mud, leaves, seeds, and grasses. These were carefully stirred and poured into child-sized aluminum cups, pans, and pie tins. After drying in the hot sun for about a day, my mud delicacies were ready to unmold and display as perfectly proportioned pretend pies and tarts fit for serving at the queen's tea, or, in our case, to our cats and dolls. With all the skills of a secret agent, I had to keep this pastime hidden from Mom. She did not approve of her girls playing in the dirt, nor did she understand or support my creativity.

Bike riding was a favorite pastime for all the Virgil kids as well. We'd ride for hours going as far as Flannery Stables, which was almost five miles away. The stables were the retirement home of the world-famous racehorse Greyhound. He was the closest we ever came to a celebrity, so it was worth the trek to see the tack room, which housed his trophies and the pictures of him proudly standing with his jockey after a victory. Then we would glance out a glass window and see Greyhound, in the flesh, grazing in the pasture.

Most of our bike riding was peaceful, fun, and uneventful except for one midsummer afternoon when I had an adventure of such intensity that it could not be duplicated on any modern-day Wii game. I was riding my bike to my grandma's and admiring the lush cornfields on one side of the road and a huge pasture containing a herd of black-and-white jersey cows on the other when a gigantic Black Angus bull with a ring in his nose noticed me and came bolting to the fence line.

The bad-tempered beast started stomping the ground with his front hooves. I was freaked out! I knew that if he jumped that fence, I would not be able to get away fast enough and his sharp-pointed horns would gore me to death. The bull started bellowing, and I felt like my heart would beat out of my chest. I was off my bike in a flash and squeezed under the fence, which was holding back the tall cornstalks.

As I fled deep into the field, I glanced back to see the enormous bull jump his fence in one giant leap. He bounded toward me and was about to charge into the cornfield when a big truck seemed to come down the road out of nowhere. The trucker began honking his horn, and that fearsome bull seemed to lose his courage as he ran away. I stayed hidden in the field for what seemed like forever, gathering my courage to leave until finally I ventured out, retrieved my bike, and made it safely home. On future rides, I always went in a different direction, and to this day I try to avoid any four-legged animal remotely resembling a cow.

Other than bike riding, I was not very athletic. Our neighbor Jerry Hardt had a baseball field next door, complete with bases and a backstop. Enough kids lived in our neighborhood to have a game at any given time. When we picked teams, I was usually picked last, which was okay with me, probably because I didn't have the same competitive spirit that some of my sisters possess.

Helen

Virgil, population 102, that's the place where I was born and raised until I reached the age of eighteen, graduated from high school, and moved out of my parents' home. That was the normal progression of a young girl's life in the forties.

I remember Virgil as a little town where everyone knew whose kid you were—a place where you could run and play with your friends and not get into any real trouble. The whole town was only equivalent to the size of a modern-day city block.

I was the oldest of five girls. I would have had an older sister, Loretta, but she died as a baby from spina bifida. There were several years between us girls and an eighteen-year span between me and my youngest sister, Anita. I was closest to my sister Ruth, who was four years my junior. Linda, Vicki, and Anita were more clustered in age.

Aunt Dell and Uncle Joe lived next door to us when I was young. Uncle Joe was my godfather, so that family was special to me. I recall my dad telling me that Uncle Joe and Aunt Dell moved to a farm in Wisconsin, and they forgot their dog Fluffy, so we would probably have to take care of him. Wow, what a lucky day! Ruth and I really loved that hairy little mutt; we would dress him in our doll clothes and take him for rides in our doll stroller. That was our very first dog, and he must have struck a special cord in our hearts because to this day we absolutely adore dogs and have always had one in our lives.

After my aunt and uncle moved away, the Hardts moved into their house. The day they moved in, my Mom gave me a Hershey bar and told me to give it to the new neighbor boy to make him feel welcome. I was a shy little girl, so I just laid it on the steps of their house, but I guess Jerry found it and got the welcoming idea because we became friends. You might say he became my best friend; we had lots of fun hanging out in Virgil.

We sometimes played with other neighborhood kids, like Elynor Turk, and her tag-along little brother, Eugene.

Genie Boy, as they called Eugene, was born with Down's syndrome, and sometimes we probably weren't nice to him. One time Mom was baking a cake, and we all wanted to lick the bowl, but she gave it to Genie Boy because he was the only one being nice. Genie Boy died when he was very young. In those days, the visitation—or wake, as they called it—was held in the deceased person's home. Now I don't recall doing this, but my mom tells me that when they were having Eugene's visitation, Jerry and I went to his house. Mom got a call on the party line saying she needed to come and get us because we were climbing in the hearse. I'm sure we were just a couple inquisitive youngsters.

Jerry's dad, Nick, owned and ran the local tavern where my Dad hung out. Nick and Dad bought a goat from one of the guys at the tavern for two dollars, thinking it would be a good pet for Jerry and me. We kept it in a pen behind our house, but it frequently escaped and ran around town. This goat was a bit feisty and had a habit of butting things and people. Actually, he wasn't a very good pet because we were afraid of him, and he wasn't too popular with the town ladies, especially when they were hanging out laundry on their wash lines and he followed right behind them to tear it down. As the tale goes, Nick and Dad had to pay that same tavern guy four bucks to take the goat back.

When my sister Ruth was old enough to play with, I was in school. Ruth was always sucking her index finger, so much so that her finger had a big bump on it. Mom was always putting nasty-tasting stuff on it to stop her habit, but then she would just suck a different finger. One day I came home from school to find Ruth on the back step with tears in her eyes. Mom had put bandages on every single finger to prevent the sucking.

I don't have a lot of photographs of when I was growing up, but one of my favorites is one of Ruth and me wearing red flower printed yellow dresses. Those dresses were sewn by Mom who was a wonderful seamstress and could create amazing clothing out of anything. The fabric was from chicken feed sacks that our grandmother gave us, but after Mom lovingly sewed them and put red rick-rack trim on to accent the dresses, they were beautiful.

We had curls in our hair that were a bit frizzy because when Mom used the curling iron, which was heated on the burner of the kitchen stove, it sometimes fried the ends of our hair. Whew, what a smell, and it was rather painful when the hot curling iron touched our scalp.

Both sets of grandparents lived on farms just outside of town, so we saw them frequently. Grandma Schmitt was the best baker around; she made tasty blonde brownies and always had a full cookie jar.

I have a fond memory of going with my Grandpa Schmitt to his cousin's greenhouse, which was several hours away. Grandpa took orders from the Virgil women for Mother's Day corsages—red carnations if your mother was deceased and pink if you still had a mom. He then picked up the flowers at the greenhouse and delivered them on Saturday, just in time for the ladies to sport them at Mass the next day. It was exciting to go with him. I sensed he was proud to introduce me to his cousin and show me all the wonderful plants in the greenhouse.

Grandpa and Grandma had thirteen children, so I had oodles of aunts and uncles. We still have large family reunions. I have so many cousins that I don't even know them all. Mom and Dad used to visit my Uncle Matt and Aunt Loretta once a month on their farm outside of town to play cards. They had three girls—Mary Lou, Dorothy, and Jane—so we had a great time on those visits. Ruth and I would love to get together with those cousins; we had a secret club, and we even kept notes. Sometimes we would do the "forbidden"—sneak into their hired man's room and look at his *Esquire* magazines with naked women. We Catholic girls had never ever seen anything like that.

My Dad's parents were a bit older. Grandpa Altepeter died when I was young; he had severe asthmatic attacks. That must have been horrible since he was a farmer. Grandma Altepeter raised chickens. It was great when she brought out her selection of feed bags, and we meticulously chose some for our clothes. Grandma was also an avid outdoor gardener; she also had lots of lush houseplants that she displayed on her sun porch. Her downstairs bathroom always had a peculiar odor because that's where she soaked eggshells in the water that she used to nourish the plants. Grandma was a saver. She had a small bedroom upstairs that was cluttered, bursting with the neatest stuff—things like balls of string, aluminum foil that she got from cigarette packages, and stacks of cardboard masks from Wheaties cereal cartons.

Grandma had seven boys. My uncles had interesting hobbies; one had a couple pet skunks that we were able to feed with caterpillars, and another uncle would sometimes catch turtles to make soup, and we would watch their severed heads continue to snap at sticks that we would put into their mouths. Behind the barn on the farm were old rusty cars that my uncles had long ago abandoned. We would work the gearshifts and pretend to be driving.

The Virgil folk had solid values. I grew up in a town where I learned good from bad, right from wrong, the merit of hard work, and the importance of family, friends, and neighbors.

Relatives

Anita

*W*hen you grow up in a small town and your parents both come from big families, there are always plenty of uncles, aunts, and cousins. Most of Mom and Dad's siblings still lived in Virgil or the surrounding farming communities. We would attend Mass with them, attend school with the cousins, and enjoy many church potlucks together.

The best time to spend with family was Sunday afternoon. After church we would go home to a lunch of pot roast and potatoes and, after changing into our play clothes, would head over to Jim's Charcoal Inn to spend the afternoon. The Charcoal Inn was the local tavern—a sort of a Cheers place where everyone knew everyone, but in Virgil, the whole family came.

The men sat around the oval wooden bar drinking beer and discussing the week's events. The women sat at tables, sipping beer or soda. They quietly exchanged recipes until their voices became almost a whisper, signifying that they had switched to gossiping about what outfit someone wore to church or how badly somebody's children had behaved. I never knew what else they talked about because whenever a child came near, they would immediately raise their voices again and start clucking about the weather or who had the best garden.

While all this activity was going on inside, the youth stepped outside, inventing our own fun. Sometimes we played tag, sometimes catch or dodge ball, if someone had remembered a ball. On a warm summer day, we'd just lie back and watch the clouds form animal shapes in the blue sky.

Inevitably, as the day wore on, the men folk would come out back to pitch horseshoes. We would then be sent inside, which was wonderful for my cousins, sisters, and me. This meant the time had come to get soda and chocolate. At Jim's, a refrigerator housed, among other things, chilled candy bars. He had quite an assortment, but my favorites were Pinwheels and Mallo Cups. Pinwheels were a round chocolate disc laden with peanuts. Indented in the chocolate were outlines making it look like a pinwheel. To make things even more tempting, the chocolate was wrapped in silver, giving an aristocratic and decadent appeal. Mallo Cups contained two cups similar in size and looked like a Reese's Peanut Butter Cup. They were made of chocolate and contained marshmallow filling with a slightly hard consistency when taken from the refrigerator, but if you let it sit a few minutes, it became gooey and pliable in your mouth. The other incentive to select Mallo Cups was because it contained a cardboard coin, ranging in value from one cent to one dollar. When you collected five dollars' worth, you sent them into the Mallo Cup Company, and they would send you four free cups via the United States Postal Service.

On an occasional Sunday when my parents didn't fellowship at the tavern, Mom would decide to visit relatives outside of Virgil. After dinner we would pile into the green Chevy four-door and head to some far-off location such as Huntley or Sycamore. These towns were less than twenty miles away, but to me the car ride seemed like forever. Being on the chunky side and always hungry, I made sure that I put lunch leftovers into my Sunday, white, patent-leather purse for the journey. Sometimes Aunt Mary and Uncle Bill would accompany us on these road trips. Aunt Mary and Uncle Bill lived five houses down from ours, theirs being right next to the general store.

Aunt Mary was a sister to Grandpa on Mom's side of the family. They did not have children, so Mom and Dad looked out for them. On the days they went with us, Mom drove their car, which was a huge black '55 Chevy that still smelled and looked new because it rarely got used. Uncle Bill had diabetes and did not drive anymore, and Aunt Mary never learned to drive, so their car sat idle unless Mom was using the car to chauffeur them somewhere.

Aunt Mary and Uncle Bill had few needs; being frugal, they had a garden in which most of their own food was grown—canning what was needed for the winter and sharing with others the excess. The general store provided milk, and another relative provided eggs. The only times they needed to go to another town was for Uncle Bill's doctor appointments or to Browns Supermarket to pick up his special order of diabetic bread. On those occasions I usually accompanied Mom as she drove them. At Browns, Uncle Bill would find his favorite treat: watermelon. Uncle Bill walked with a cane so he could not carry the melon. I also loved watermelon, so I was always honored to walk with him to the produce area and carry the largest melon we could find. I could barely wait till we got back to their house and Aunt Mary would slice us both a huge piece and put it in a metal pie dish. We would both be exiled to the backyard bench and forced to tuck a towel into our shirt collar so we would not make a mess. Being careful to pick out the seeds so a watermelon did not grow in my stomach, I savored every juicy bite until the pan was depleted of the red succulent fruit.

The other joy in Uncle Bill's life was picking up hickory nuts in the local farm pastures. Mom, Uncle Bill, Aunt Mary, me, and any other sister Mom forced to would drive to a relative's farm and crawl through the barbed wire fence into the pasture filled with live cows and fresh manure. Being careful not to step in the newly laid fertilizer, we would find a hickory nut tree and fill large cloth potato sacks full of nuts. This event happened four or five times during a season until Uncle Bill had enough nuts stored in his work shed to last the winter. He would then spend all fall cracking the nuts and sorting them into glass jars he would give to all the relatives for use at Christmas for cookies and nut bread. As he got older, his eyesight weakened, and oftentimes you would bite into a treat and find a hickory nutshell he had overlooked in his sorting process. It seemed to me like part of the charm and just a reminder of his hard work.

Aunt Mary and Uncle Bill appeared somewhat mean and stern because they never had children. Uncle Bill wore a hearing aid, and oftentimes he did not hear what was being said to him. I personally believe he sometimes chose to turn it off so he did not have to listen to Aunt Mary. He spent most of his days sitting on the back bench sorting his hickory nuts or whittling sticks with his mean little dog barking and growling at anyone who got close. Uncle Bill also chewed tobacco and spit it onto the ground frequently.

Aunt Mary was a sturdy, quite homely German woman. Her face was weathered and wrinkled, and she had a slight mustache. Most times you'd find her sitting on the front porch watching the cars go by and gossiping on the phone with another family member. She particularly liked to talk with my grandmother because they both were strong-willed women, and many times they'd fight over something such as the date of someone's birth or death. Ultimately, this led to Aunt Mary pulling out her box of obituary cards and proving herself right or admitting that Grandma had won this round.

Being the youngest, I never seemed to get enough attention at home, but the door was always open at their house. Getting off the school bus, I would jet to the porch at Aunt Mary's and show her the latest fashion in finger-painting or clay modeling. She would praise my work, and we would proceed to the back room, where she displayed it on the wall. This room was used for doing the laundry and housed the washboard, washtubs, and the electric wringer washer that was her pride and joy. She always explained, as she hung my latest masterpiece, how she would enjoy looking at it on Monday washday. She had some cookies ready as a snack for me, and on special days she had her specialty, frosted creams. Frosted creams were a molasses brownie with a thin layer of powdered-sugar frosting. Nobody in all of Virgil made the recipe like Aunt Mary, and to this day I still don't know of any one who can master this treat.

Vicki

Yes, we had plenty of relatives. That brings my thoughts to the Schmitt family reunion. This event was extremely important to my mother, who would visit with her sisters and brothers, plus show off her children, grandchildren, and great-grandchildren. Not making it to the family reunion was not acceptable, and if you didn't, you had better have a darn good excuse!

I was a shy child, and this was not an exciting event for me. I became easily bored, hanging on my parents, begging, "Can we go home now?" Of course, my mother, being an outgoing person and definitely a family-oriented individual, would continue to try to convince me how much fun I might have. I became thoroughly embarrassed as she dragged me off to introduce me to one of my other bored cousins so I could hang out with them—neither of us being too thrilled with this. The highlight of the day was lunch, served exactly at noon right after prayer. It usually consisted of hotdogs, beef and ham, every type of salad you would think of—from green bean casserole to fruit salads—chips, etc. Uncle Pat would never disappoint us as each year he brought fresh cheese and sausage from Wisconsin. And for the grand finale— the desserts! There were so many sugary delicacies that you couldn't just try one. The Schmitt side of the family is known for their baking skills. Most of the family contributed to the *Vittles from Virgil* cookbook, produced by the Altar and Rosary Society in Virgil. And don't forget the beverages—beer, orange drink, and lemonade. Games of baseball and volleyball followed lunch, and quite often, a battle with water and water balloons would ensue with all the kids getting wet at the end of the day.

In the past few years, the reunions have moved to my Uncle John and Aunt Diane's home. Less people attend now because many of the sisters and brothers have passed away, including my mother. I have grown to understand why the reunions were so important to my mother, and I do my best to attend every year, continuing the tradition of forcing children and grandchildren to attend. By the time they have reached my age, hopefully they will find the importance of the family reunion too.

The most colorful of all the Schmitt relatives were my great-aunt Mary and great-uncle Bill, who lived right next to the Country Store. We spent many hours playing rummy, picking raspberries, collecting apples for applesauce, and shelling the hickory nuts we collected from local trees. Picking up the hickory nuts was always interesting as we had to go into cow pastures. I kept a close eye on those cows and also the cow pies. It was a lot of work shelling the nuts and also watching for those gross little white worms who liked the nuts too.

Aunt Mary had raspberry bushes behind her house. We loved the fresh raspberries, especially atop a bowl of vanilla ice cream. Picking raspberries was hard work, getting in between the thorny bushes to pull off the luscious fruit and always getting bitten by the mosquitoes. Still they were worth it. Yum!

Aunt Mary also had apple trees. The years when the apples were especially good, we picked them up from the ground and peeled and sliced them. Some would be frozen for later use. Others would be made into fresh apple pies and apple crisp. Mom would also make applesauce using a special pan with a blade and handle. You could cook your apples without having to peel them. You put them into this device, and it would *smush* the apples into a sauce, leaving the peel behind for disposal. She then added the sugar and cinnamon, and the applesauce was frozen for future use. The bad part about the apple trees was the worms and having to pick them up before mowing the lawn or they would get caught in the mower blade.

Uncle Bill loved to fish, so we would often go to a place called Berryland. There was a swimming pool we kids were allowed to cool off in, and Aunt Mary and Uncle Bill fished in the surrounding ponds. Sometimes I fished with them too. I remember fishing the pond a distance from Aunt Mary and Uncle Bill when my mom approached me. She said, "Your Uncle Bill was telling me about a little girl with ponytails just down the pond from him who could really cast a line. I looked, and it was you!" She was so proud of me, and it made me proud too. The only kind of fish we ever caught were bullheads—a kind of disgusting fish that looks like it has a mustache. Aunt Mary or Uncle Bill would take the fish off the hook, as the mustaches could sting us. They actually took the fish home, gutted them, and cooked them. Okay, fishing can be fun, but count me out on the rest of it. I can still remember seeing my aunt and uncle lay out the newspaper and clean the fish. *Ewwww!*

Linda

Every Sunday morning started out with picking out your best dress and going to Sunday Mass. We would put on our chapel veils, and Mother would have a beautiful flowered hat. On Easter Sunday, we would always get a new Easter hat, gloves, and a purse!

Mom came from a family of thirteen, and Dad came from a family of eight, so we always had someone to visit and plenty of cousins to play games with. Our families are close, and to this day, every year, we have a family reunion on my mother's side of the family.

Great-Aunt Mary and Uncle Bill lived right down the street, so when we got bored or lonely, they were always more than willing to entertain us. Aunt Mary made oatmeal for lunch, and then we played 500 Rummy or Brains, which was like today's game of Concentration. They even had a card shuffler! Sometimes I helped Aunt Mary clean, and she would always find some treasure she was willing to part with and give it to me. She had some rather interesting things, one of which was a head you would put string in and the string would come out of it's mouth. She collected cards that she reused simply by pasting a piece of paper over the original sender's name and replacing it with her name. Aunt Mary also had a beautiful china cabinet filled with sparkling glass goblets and other expensive-looking glassware. Mom inherited the cabinet, and it became her most prized possession.

Aunt Mary had many friends, so she decided she would like them to have certain items to remember her by. She instructed her friends and us kids to pick something we liked, and she wrote our name on a piece of adhesive tape and put it on the bottom of the article. After Aunt Mary passed away, people told my mom that Mary said they could have an item, and, lo and behold, their name was on the bottom of the item in question. I have a beautiful-cut glass cruet that was my chosen prize. Aunt Mary also used to crochet and tat. She made handkerchiefs and pillowcases she would give as wedding and shower gifts. I wish I had paid more attention and learned to master those skills.

Aunt Mary and Uncle Bill drove us to school in the morning because they always attended daily Mass. We would get to Route 64—the busiest road in Virgil—and Uncle Bill would look to the left and Aunt Mary would look to the right and say, "Step on it, Bill!" and we would go flying across Route 64. Sometimes I think I might have been safer walking.

Once a week, Dad and I would go mow Aunt Mary's lawn. Dad would go around the hard parts, and I did the rest. I can remember mowing in the back of her yard under the apple trees. Apples, and the bugs on them, came shooting out the back of the lawnmower, landing on my legs. I also mowed the lawn at home. Looking back, no wonder I was a little mean—I did all the work!

Ruth

Unlike my sisters, my memories of Aunt Mary (Tanta Mary, as Mom called her) were not as pleasant. I considered her to be a crabby, meddlesome busybody.

Aunt Mary and Uncle Bill lived on a big old farm in Maple Park—about five miles from Virgil—before moving to the house next to the store. They had a large, black farm dog named Blackie that took his meals behind the cook stove in their kitchen. Blackie was bad-tempered and not accustomed to being around children, so I was warned not to pet him, especially while he was eating. Of course, as a child, I did not always listen, so I lovingly pet him during one of his feedings, and he bit me badly. Bleeding and with tears streaming down my face, I went to Aunt Mary for first-aid and comfort. I was rebuked instead of being soothed; she said, "Ruthie, it's your own fault! Next time, listen to me."

Another time when I jokingly accused her of stealing some pork chops from the butcher shop, she became irate and demanded a full-out apology. Even after I dutifully apologized at Mom's insistence, Aunt Mary still proceeded to lecture me for what seemed like hours. I really was ashamed of the joke; however, her persistence in mentioning it often helped me to justify the joke.

Those moments paled in comparison to the horror of what was about to come. After Aunt Mary and Uncle Bill moved to Virgil, Aunt Mary became the self-ordained town busybody. Sitting on a couch on her front porch, she observed everything. Entering or leaving Virgil was not possible without going past her house. Upon our family returning from a trip to town, she would call and find out where we had been. She could also tell you when and where all the neighbors had gone because she also called them and asked. Even though she busied herself with meddling into everyone's lives, she always made special time for our family, delighting, especially, in observing me, hoping to find a tidbit of gossip. We all caught the bus to high school in front of her house, so she always knew if we were not on the bus in the morning, and she immediately called Mom to see if we overslept, had been sick, or what else might have caused this offense.

Her eagle eyes also saw everything we were doing while waiting for the bus, which she promptly reported back to our mother. One morning, my boyfriend, John—who later became my husband—waited at the store for me. Rather than board the school bus, I jumped into his green 1950 Oldsmobile. I blissfully spent the day with him, returning in the afternoon at the exact time the bus pulled up to the store. Feeling pretty proud of this deception, I walked home carrying a stack of schoolbooks. Having been alerted by my nemesis, Aunt Mary, Mom waited furiously at the kitchen door for me. She was not only upset with me for my behavior but also because she didn't like Aunt Mary to know our family business. My punishment was forbidding me to see John again. Mom said that things were moving too fast with us because I was only fourteen and John was nineteen, but it was too late to stop us. In the future, I learned to be more careful, and I would sneak out of the house to meet John at the Catholic Church, which was out of range to Aunt Mary's prying eyes. Incidentally, I eloped and married John when I was eighteen. We have recently celebrated our forty- ninth wedding anniversary. I am sure Aunt Mary is still up in heaven watching me and reporting to Mom my every move.

Unlike Aunt Mary, my Grandma Altepeter raised a large family and knew how to handle her grandchildren. She lived about a mile down the road from us on a large farm. She was a character, and I dearly loved her. She enjoyed the outdoors and kept a bountiful vegetable garden and an enormous flower garden. She instilled her passion for flowers in me as we spent many happy hours working among her perennials and breathing in the fragrance of their many blossoms. Grandma saved eggshells, which she put in quart jars and covered with water. After sitting for about a week, this water became a potion for her houseplants. The potion must have worked, because her plants were always gorgeous.

She had to keep her gardens fenced because the chickens she raised loved to enter the garden and make a mess. The laying hens were confined to the chicken house. She allowed her guinea fowl, bandy hens and roosters, and leghorn hens with chicks to roam freely. Seeing seven or eight hens followed by a brood of fluffy yellow or black chicks in the yard eating grass or catching bugs was common. At night, I would help her round up the little families and lock each hen with her chicks in individual chicken coops that looked like miniature A-frame houses. There they were protected from any nocturnal predators that might be searching for a tasty evening snack.

Sometimes we would find a nest of eggs in the yard or in the tall grass. Grandma would take these eggs into her house to candle them to determine if they had been fertilized. She would enter into a small, completely dark closet and put the egg at one end of a hard paper cylinder and hold the other cylinder end to a light bulb. She turned the light on to see if the egg was fertilized; we could see the tiny chick being formed and moving inside the egg. How amazing! Sort of like an early day ultrasound. She always carefully and lovingly returned the fertilized eggs to the exact spot where she found them so the hen would return and hatch them.

My parents were thrifty, but my Grandma Altepeter was the "Queen of Thrift." She had a walk-in food pantry where, in addition to food staples, she kept and saved balls of string, foil from sticks of gum, and all sizes of rubber bands. She hoarded every imaginable type of coupon and box top she found. Many expired, but she never had the heart to throw any of them away. She saved any and all prizes that came in boxes of food or detergent. She valued anything from the little paper or plastic trinkets in Cracker Jacks to the glasses and dishes that came in detergent boxes. She had a room upstairs where she kept these treasures, and they often became our birthday or Christmas gifts.

My childhood memories play host to many other special relatives—Dad's brothers: Uncle Willie, who kept a pet skunk; Uncle Joe, who raised parakeets in his basement and gave a bright-blue bungee named Herbie to Helen; and Uncle Henry, who worked at the junkyard. Uncle Phil had been accidentally shot during a bank robbery in Virgil, but he did not die from the gunshot— he died when a ceiling beam in the barn fell on his head.

Mom's family consisted of Grandma Schmitt, who, every evening, sat in her rocking chair and recited her rosary before bed, and Grandpa Schmitt, who paid me and Pug, his dog, a nickel for each barn rat we caught and killed. We did a great job sometimes catching as many as five rats a day. Mom's siblings were: Aunt Esther, who called me "Foofy", Aunt Sis, who called me "Ruby", and Aunt Loretta who always served Ginger Ale and whose house smelled like a bakery. Aunt Clara, married my Uncle Chuck and bore and raised fourteen children. Uncle Bob, crushed a baby bird in my hand; and Uncle John, was and still is the handsomest man I'd ever seen.

I had even more aunts and uncles than I have mentioned here. I have fond memories of each and every one of them. We sisters have been surrounded with caring relatives, not perfect by any means, but they all blended perfectly into our family. How blessed we were to be a part of this big and loving family!

Helen

I could certainly fill many pages with stories about my relatives since Dad came from a family of eight and Mom from a family of thirteen. All of my Dad's siblings were boys—can you imagine eight boys? They were a rather rowdy bunch,known to drink a little too much alcohol. Grandma always had a bottle of Mogen David wine,which she served in fancy little goblets on special occasions. She also had an ample supply of apple cider made from the apples in her orchard.

My Grandpa Altepeter died when I was young, and a couple of my uncles lived with Grandma, probably to help with the farming.

After my Uncle Phil was shot in the hip in a bank robbery, it took a long time for him to recover. He lived at home but needed more help than Grandma was capable of providing. Grandma's brother was a priest, and he had a divorced parishioner with three children who needed lodging. She moved into Grandma's house to help care for Uncle Phil. Well, wouldn't you know it, Uncle Phil fell in love with her, and they got married. This became somewhat of a scandal in the family because, first of all, divorce is forbidden to Catholics and to marry a person who is divorced is right up there with the worst of sins. I didn't even know a divorced person before this woman came on the scene.

Grandma Altepeter was the first person I knew who had a TV because Uncle Phil, being bedridden for a while, needed good entertainment. However, there weren't programs on all day like now, and you were lucky to find a program on more than one of the three channels at a time. The TV had horrible reception, the TV stars looked like they were in a snowstorm, and of course it was only in black and white. My family would look forward to the mile walk down the gravel road to Grandma's place to watch the *Ed Sullivan Show* with the June Taylor dancers. Grandma thought it shameful how scantily clad they were. Modesty is a virtue. It has been rumored that one of my aunts (by marriage) wore a two-piece bathing suit on her honeymoon. How daring!

Families had a lot of pride and patriotism. Three of my uncles were in the military service. Both of my grandmothers proudly displayed photos of them in their uniforms.

Another thing that made our family bust their buttons was if one of their children had a vocation to become a priest or a nun. As I mentioned, Grandma had a brother who became a priest, and I had two cousins on the other side who had a calling. Mary Lou became a Franciscan nun and Jerry a monk. I recall Jerry as just a young boy when he made his own little altar with statues of Mary and Jesus that he could pray to.

A few of my mom's younger sisters were in high school when I entered grade school. I really admired them. They were so beautiful. Aunt Esther was a cheerleader, and Aunt Jean had the most beautiful black hair, as did my Aunt Sissy. I credit those aunts for the fondness I have for the music from the forties. I'm sure it's because I heard my party girl aunts play their favorites over and over again.

However, it was not all fun and games. There were times when my aunts and uncles would gather at Grandma and Grandpa Schmitt's to work in the fields, picking corn or baling hay. They also put up provisions for the winter months. I remember watching them cut up heads of cabbage and store it in huge crocks. They mixed salt in with the cabbage and left it to age into sauerkraut. We kids would sometimes sneak into the basement where the crocks were stored. They were covered with large white cloths while the cabbage fermented. We would carefully slip our hands under the cloths and take samples of the salty mixture to snack on. I guess our little stomachs were strong because I don't remember getting a bellyache.

I most vividly recall when they butchered chickens—not for the faint of heart. They chopped the heads of the chickens off, and those creatures would flop around with blood flying everywhere. It was downright scary, and I can almost smell the stench of wet chicken feathers when they dipped them into scalding hot water to pick the feathers off. When you see the chicken breasts, wings, etc., all wrapped in cellophane at Hy-Vee, don't you wonder how the kids of today think they got there?

Most of my aunts and uncles stayed close to Virgil when they grew up, but a few left for faraway places like Wisconsin and Indiana. Every year there would be a big family reunion at Grandma and Grandpa Schmitt's farm. It is the only day that everyone gets together at the same time. This is a tradition that is still carried on today at the home of Uncle John and Aunt Diane.

There seems to be one memory that all of us sisters treasure, picking up hickory nuts with Aunt Mary and Uncle Bill. They were actually our great-aunt and great-uncle, but we were all close to them. As Uncle Bill aged, his sight began to fail, and you had to be very careful to not chomp down on a shell that he might have accidently missed and got into the jar. Uncle Bill was diabetic, and he craved sweet things. He was known to have a wad of several sticks of sugarless gum in his mouth at one time. He also had a rather gross habit of chewing tobacco and spitting it in a tin can by his chair.

My Great-Grandma Schmitt lived with Aunt Mary and Uncle Bill when she was very old—well into her nineties. Her poor eyesight caused her to wear thick glasses, but she and Aunt Mary did beautiful, intricate tatting around handkerchiefs. I often wish I had paid more attention and learned that skill.

We sisters have some pretty healthy genes that we inherited from our sturdy German ancestors, but some of us got the asthma gene. Grandpa Altepeter had it; he used whiskey to help him breathe. Nicky Schmitt—my mom's brother—died at the age of twelve from it. Vicki and I are the sisters who have inherited that trait.

Going to School

Anita

*E*veryone in Virgil, except the two Protestant families, sent their children to S.S. Peter and Paul Catholic grade school. The building—located on Meredith Road, right in the center of town next to the church rectory—was the school in which we were taught by the Franciscan Order of Nuns. The school housed first through eighth grades in four classrooms, so first and second were taught together, third and fourth together, etc.

At six years old, I first experienced education through the eyes of Sister Mary Anne—a short, stout nun with a permanent scowl on her face. I had attended kindergarten at the public school in Maple Park and was always entertained. I rode the bus that picked me up at the general store and, upon arriving at the school, was greeted every afternoon by a young, vibrant teacher who always had a big smile on her face. After getting our backpacks put away, we would color, sing, play, and take naps on our little rugs. The half-day outing, occurring for an entire school year, did not get me ready for grade school like experts seem to think it should.

On the first day of school at S.S. Peter and Paul, I arrived in my new dress. Most of my clothing was hand-me-downs from an older sister or cousin, but not today. Mom had made me a new dress from fabric she had left over from another of her many sewing creations. The multicolored flowered dress touched the floor when I knelt. She explained to me that the nuns always did dress check the first day and the hemline must touch the floor when I knelt or I would be in big trouble. Also, no sleeveless clothing would be allowed and, of course, no pants or shorts.

I was now a young Catholic lady formed in the image of our Virgin Mary. Boys were expected to wear dress pants and a shirt tucked in, along with a belt. I watched in horror as two of the boys who had been wrestling on the way to school did not pass inspection. Sister called them to the front of the class and said they were a disgrace to God and proceeded to tuck their shirts in for them as if they were two years old. After this humiliation, we all lined up so we could walk quickly without talking to church for morning Mass. Girls were told to put on their chapel veils since we could not enter the Lord's house with our heads bare.

We all knew how to behave in church since we had been attending since the day we were born, so this was uneventful. After church, it was single-file back to our classroom so the sister could start our lessons. Reading, writing, arithmetic, and catechism filled every day, along with a short lunch and recess time. Silence in class, unless you raised your hand and had been called upon, was the norm. It was at school that I learned how to become a proper young lady, not asking questions or forming my own opinions. Sister Mary Anne was there to give me my opinions if needed.

Discipline had been a major component of any Catholic education, and our school was no exception. Schoolwork would be done completely, accurately, and silently in the classrooms. I had always been a good student, so this did not create a problem for me, but several boys and one girl struggled with their studies. Daily, they were subjected to the ridicule and berating from the nun. If one of them wrote a letter upside down, she would stand them on their head, holding their feet in the air, until they apologized. If their penmanship was not neat, or if they had too many incorrect answers or did not finish the assignments, they would be sent to the corner for the remainder of the period. If someone dared to talk back to Sister Mary Anne, they would be called to the front of the class and made to hold out their hand as she slapped the top of it with a wooden, double-edged metal ruler, standard issue to all the nuns. This pattern continued for me through sixth grade, with the exception of Sister Mary Anne retiring to the Old Nuns' Home and being replaced by Sister Mary Albert during my third-grade year. Sister Mary Albert was younger than Sister Mary Anne and, by those standards, just as mean.

At some point, the Franciscan nuns had been allowed to change their habit. They were now allowed to wear black knee-length dresses with a white blouse and a black jacket or sweater over it. I remember the first day Sister

Mary Albert stood in front of our class, with her feet together and her back as straight as a chair. All I could notice were her bowlegs jutting out from under her dress. I immediately thought to myself that she should have stayed with the floor-length dress. Wanting to laugh, I caught myself, fearing I would be called to the front of the room to explain what was so humorous. I would then be sent to the priest for confession and have to pray a rosary instead of the usual punishment he handed out: three Our Fathers and three Hail Marys. After that, I would be sent home to be further punished by my parents. The punishment never fit the crime, but that was just the way it was growing up Catholic.

Seventh grade brought on a quite unsettling change. They announced the Diocese was going to close down our school after this year because we were not financially able to maintain it. We would all be transferred to public school the next year. As if that was not bad enough, we had a new male teacher, Mr. Bernard, and he was not even a Catholic. He expected us to participate in class and even asked for our opinions. I was sure this bordered on heresy.

One particular lesson has stayed with me all these years. During a science class, he started talking about his belief in Darwin and the theory of evolution. I knew this was not in the approved Catholic curriculum, so I sat silently, praying that God would forgive him of these horrible lies of Satan he was spreading. He asked for our opinions, and no one dared say anything. Dropping the subject, he went on with whatever the real lesson happened to be. That day stuck in my mind all year. As a Catholic, I felt I had let God down. I should have raised my hand and told him what our catechism said about creation, but I was afraid. At the end of the school year, I wrote him a letter explaining how God created the world and I had forgiven him for his lies because, since he was not a Catholic, he did not understand what he was saying.

Many adults have bad memories of Catholic education and treatment students received at the hands of the sisters. I can appreciate these sentiments, but for me I feel I received a first-rate education that has helped me to become the person I am today.

Vicki

Nita was the first of us to attend kindergarten. To this day she holds this over our heads, saying she is smarter than any of us because she is a kindergarten graduate. Yeah, whatever!

But anyway, first grade was my first experience being away from home for a whole day. I never got into trouble at school, mostly because I was afraid to—I was shy. I loved coloring, doing any kind of art project, and I was an excellent speller. As I progressed into second and third grade, I helped the first graders with their reading and other assignments. I enjoyed this, and I also got out of some of my other classes while helping.

One day while playing dodge ball on the playground with the other girls, I glanced to my left and saw an orange-haired, freckle-faced man approaching me. I freaked, ran to my sister Linda, and jumped onto her back, expecting her to save me. One of the nuns, noticing what was going on, dragged me up to the man and introduced me. It turned out he was a lay teacher, but being shy and only expecting to see nuns, I feared he was a kidnapper or murderer. He tried to befriend me by taking me inside and letting me ring the recess bell, but I was still skeptical he belonged at our school.

I realize now that in Catholic school we had different terminology for things. For example, we had a cloakroom—a room with hooks and shelves for hanging your coats. We also had book bags—not backpacks. We drank from a bubbler—known today as a water fountain. We had a lunch box with a thermos. The thermos was lined with glass and was easily broken as the lunch box was made of metal, except for the plastic handle.

We did not have a lunch program at our school, so everyone carried a lunch box. We were able to buy milk—sometimes white and sometimes chocolate—and quite often I remember it being spoiled. You always shook your milk when you chose it to make sure there was movement in the liquid. Milk only cost a couple of cents for the half-pint carton.

Class sizes at our school were small, each classroom generally containing two classes, and we stayed in the same room for the entire day. I believe this resulted in a good education. There was no way you could get away without getting your schoolwork done or answering questions in class. My eighth-grade graduation class consisted of eight people. I was shocked going from this size school to Kaneland High School. My high school graduating class consisted of 129 kids, still small by today's standards but huge to me at the time.

Linda

I loved summer, but soon it would end and school would begin.

The nuns seemed to play favorites, and no matter how hard I tried, I was not one of the chosen ones. Some of the kids' older siblings or parents would help them and practically do their projects or homework for them. Mom pretty much made us do our homework and projects by ourselves. While the other kids got A++, I usually got a C. Once I got a D on my report card in Religion, and one of my older sisters severely scolded me and said it was totally unacceptable. Of all subjects, how could I get a D in the most important one—*Religion?*

We always started school by going to Mass first. You had to fast at least three hours before going to Holy Communion, so Mom would pack us cinnamon toast wrapped in foil for breakfast to be eaten at school after Mass. Usually about five minutes before Mass ended, I would get sick and have to leave church or sit down in the pew. I think I was having anxiety attacks because I was so afraid of not performing up to the nun's expectations.

Despite my fear of the nuns, for some odd reason, I always wanted to be a nun. I would dress up as a nun, wearing a homemade costume consisting of a veil and rosary. Some of my favorite movies were *The Singing Nun, Bernadette of Lourdes*, and *The Nun's Story.*

I was quiet and hated to be noticed or have any individual attention given to me at school. To my

dismay, everything was done in alphabetical order—
seating, attendance, and announcing your quiz grade
so the nun could record it in her grade book. (*Oh no!
It was going to go in my permanent record!*) My name
was Linda Altepeter, so I was always first. To top
that off, I was the shortest in my class. . Whenever
we had processions in church, they would line us up
according to height. You guessed it, first again! For
Communion we would kneel on these special padded
velvet kneelers. The priest said since I was so short he
wanted me to stand so he didn't have to bend down so
far to give me Communion.

When I started high school, I realized I was actually
a very intelligent individual. I did get a good education
in Catholic school, but I was also robbed of the joy
associated with learning.

I'm glad my happiness didn't revolve around
my school life. Outside of school, I felt loved and
appreciated, retaining my Pollyanna attitude.

I was always glad when summer came because
Catholic schools didn't have summer school.

Ruth

Just like my other sisters, Helen and I attended the
Catholic grade school. We were taught by Franciscan
nuns in long black dresses called *habits* with white,
starched collars that looked like big round bibs. Their
habits were topped off with black veils held on by
white fabric, which completely covered their heads
down to their eyebrows. This caused me to wonder

if they indeed had any hair at all or if maybe all nuns were actually bald-headed ladies. Perhaps this was the reason they became nuns and possibly why they were always crabby.

Helen and I started school in the original building, which was later torn down and replaced by the new, larger structure. Our schoolhouse had only two classrooms. The little room housed first through fourth grade (no kindergarten for us back then). The big room had fifth through eighth grades. We had two indoor restrooms— one for girls and one for boys. We also had a cloakroom for our coats and lunches, an auditorium, and an extra room where the better students could instruct those who needed tutoring.

When I got my work done early, I took both Peanuts Keifer and Leon Petit to the extra room to study reading or practice spelling. Mostly we would talk, pretending to study if someone walked past our door. Peanuts was famous for the time he tied Sister Mary Alisha's shoelaces together while being punished by sitting under her desk, which she called her "doghouse." In class, he usually messed around or tried to climb the pipes or crawl into the venting system.

Because our family lived only a mile from school, we usually rode our bikes or walked with other neighbor kids. Students had to bring their lunches in bags or boxes and eat at their desks unless they were one of the lucky ones who got to go home for lunch, like Helen and me. At exactly noon, our Mom would be parked and waiting in front of school. Helen and I would rush out as soon as the lunch bell rang so we'd have time to get home and eat Mom's wonderful cooking.

When we arrived home, she would have our lunch waiting on the table. We often had fried egg or grilled cheese sandwiches, accompanied by steaming-hot Tomato or Chicken noodle soup. We also loved bread-n-butter waffles made from slices of buttered bread dipped in an egg and milk mixture and cooked in a waffle iron. Helen was a neat eater, but I was a little sloppy , therefore, had to wear a big ole plastic bib so I wouldn't spill on my school dress. One time I thoroughly embarrassed myself by walking back into the classroom still wearing my bib. Another time, on the way back to school, a big black crow flew overhead and dropped a giant, white, runny gob of poop on me. Mom had to rush me home and clean me up.

One of the highlights of our school year was the Christmas pageant in which the entire student body participated. We proudly presented this program to our parents and family the night before Christmas vacation began. Preparations for this annual event started about six weeks earlier with auditions for the play. I usually got a speaking role, being the only girl in my class of six, and there was always a need for a mother or sisters. In addition, I had a very loud voice, which could be heard all the way to the back seats of the auditorium. Kids who didn't win a role in the play could be assured a spot in the Nativity scene. Extra shepherds were always needed clad in their dads' striped bathrobes, along with some angels with tinsel halos, cotton-balled sheep, cows, and donkeys. The most coveted roles of Mary and Joseph usually went to some kids who were lucky enough to have a baby brother or sister the right size and temperament to play Baby Jesus in the manger.

Following the play, all students, regardless of their ability to carry a tune, sang Christmas Carols while waiting for the arrival of Santa. I remember one Christmas when Santa, who, over the years, was played by various dads and uncles, stopped off at the local tavern and lost track of time. We kids had to sing and sing, repeating those carols many times over until someone fetched Santa and brought him staggering into our midst. That Christmas, Santa smelled of stale cigarettes and whiskey, but he was still special to us. After Santa's arrival, all the children filed past him one at a time to receive our yearly gifts. We looked forward to our annual red mesh stocking filled with nuts, apples, and a big juicy orange. Our special delight was the colorful rectangular cardboard box with a wide white string handle crammed full of hard candy that was usually melted or stuck together into one big glob.

After graduating from eighth grade, all of us Sisters attended public high school. Kids who we considered rich got to go to private Catholic schools—Marmion for the boys and Madonna for the girls—but we were not in that elite category. A new public school called Kaneland had just been built out in the country in the middle of a cornfield, and my class was the first to attend. To get to Kaneland, you had to take the school bus. I stayed up most of the night before school, worrying about how to get on the bus. It was my first bus ride, and I couldn't have been more nervous if I had been taking a shuttle to the moon.

I had a lot of hang-ups—like my fear of those scary little people who lived in the walls at our home, the guys who peeked in our windows at night, and people who might be hiding down in a dark corner of our basement or way deep back in Mom's walk-in closet. Although the dark of night was a fearsome thing , getting on the bus early in the morning on the first day of high school put me in a panic. Somehow, by the grace of God, I managed to board the big yellow bus and get to school unharmed.

Once I got to school, I was confronted by a combination lock keeping me from accessing my assigned locker. Another freshman who had his wits about him showed me how to work the mysterious lock. Soon I had put all my school supplies in my own personal locker. Feeling pretty proud of my accomplishment, I closed my locker with a big heave and slammed my pinkie finger in the door. The pain was excruciating, and I promptly fainted right there in the school hall. The next thing I remembered was waking up in the nurse's station. Within a half hour, my Mom arrived to take me home, thus ending my first day of high school.

The following school days did get better. I made friends and learned how to get around in a large school. The cafeteria, with its hot lunch menu, was a treat to me, although I was a little shocked to see that spaghetti came with a red tomato sauce covering it. Our mom always cooked plainly with no sauces and few spices. At our home, spaghetti came only with butter. Kids would put catsup, mustard, even relish on their hamburgers. What a surprise for someone who always ate her sandwiches plain!

Speaking of surprises, it was more like a huge shock to realize that we were expected to take nude showers with all the girls in our physical education class. Our little country grade school did not offer P.E., and the nuns would have never condoned any type of communal showering.

All in all, my school experiences—both Catholic and public—were eye-opening, broadening, and a wonderful preparation for the time I would be grown up and ready to leave the comfort and safety of my home in Virgil.

Helen

I absolutely loved school! I liked learning and was a good student. I listened obediently, which is what the nuns liked—conformity. My first learning experience outside the home was first grade at St. Peter and Paul School. Sister Mary Alicia was my teacher, my idol.

I remember her as a looming figure dressed in her long black garb with the black veil and stiff white material framing her face. I later found out she was only four feet ten inches tall, but to a short kid, she appeared big. The nuns' garb had big sleeves, and they kept all sorts of stuff in them—things they took from the bad kids. We heard that nuns didn't have hair, so it was always puzzling when a wisp of hair escaped from under that white material. All the girls in my class wanted to be nuns when we grew up, but we reconsidered when someone told us we would have to pray all day long.

The school was a part of the whole parish. The building was right next to the church and the priest's house. The nuns' house was just across the street. We always had three nuns—one to teach the first through fourth grades that were housed in one school room, one to educate the fifth through eighth grades in another room. The third was an old nun who was what we termed the "cook sister"; she took care of the household chores in the nuns' house.

When I was in fifth grade, a new sister was assigned to the school, Sister Mary Samuel. She was great at drawing. One time she drew a picture of the cook sister in pastel chalk—it looked just like her. Art was not always emphasized at St. Peter and Paul's school, so it was a real treat to have a nun with such creative and artistic talent. The real head of the school was Father Esser. He only came over when it was time to pass out the report cards. He would sit at the nun's desk and call out the student's name, scrutinizing the grades while the student stood in front of the whole class. How embarrassing was that? I always got good grades, so I was excited when he came to the school, but there were some students who probably absolutely dreaded his presence.

Father Esser was extremely dramatic; he would pound on the pulpit when giving a sermon in church, and his face would turn bright red as he preached about the wrath of God. He took advantage and made an example of every unfortunate local occurrence to point out the sins of the flesh.

That brings me to a scary event—a Catholic girl's first confession. We practiced telling our sins to the nun before we actually went into the dark little cubbyhole called the confessional; you might call it a dress rehearsal. In the confessional, there was a little sliding window that Father Esser pushed back when it was your turn. It was dark, but I feared that if he knew who I was, he would yell at me for being so evil, maybe even make an example of me in the next sermon. I get a little short of breath just writing about the whole experience.

I remember high school as being both a frightening and exciting experience. I had to ride a bus to a neighboring town—Maple Park—and I went from a class size of five to a class of twenty, and most of them were *not* Catholics. I didn't know any of those kids, and most of them had been classmates with each other since the first grade. This was foreign territory; different subjects—no Catechism, no Bible History, no nuns, no friends, and gym was a requirement. A few things stick out in my mind as lifesavers. I kind of played the piano—well, enough to accompany the chorus—I was good at English, a fast typist, and we had an opportunity to take dance lessons.

I had a part-time job as a carhop during my last two years of high school. This was in a different town, and much of my spare time was spent working and hanging out with the young folk in that town. Consequently, I didn't become close with my own classmates, but I enjoy attending the class reunions, and I often wish I would have gotten to know them better.

I graduated from Maple Park High School with excellent grades and obtained a scholarship to attend college at Northern Illinois University in DeKalb. I went for just a few months and then quit. I was told girls don't need college because they'll just get married and raise kids.

What Kind of Vacation Is This?

Anita

My parents were frugal people. I think having lived through the Great Depression, they understood the value of money and importance of never spending cash on frivolous things. They also never bought anything on credit. Vacations were considered a waste of time and funds. Instead of traveling, the family would be allowed to purchase something Mom considered a luxury. One year, the family received a RCA color console television for the living room; another year, it was a room air conditioner; and another year, it was a new carpet for the dining area.

While the parents thought upgrading our home with useful items was wonderful, I always felt like I was being cheated out of some grand adventure. The neighbors on both sides of our house would depart Virgil for a two-week vacation every summer. The families rented the same cabins each year in the great Wisconsin wilderness of Rhinelander on the beautiful Eagle River. For months before the event, they would talk about little else. The boys spent hours outside practicing their casting skills so they would be ready to snag a most impressive bass. The girls would be chatting incessantly about the beach or out shopping with their moms, buying a new swimsuit and sandals and making sure they had everything ready for the cabin. By May, the adults had already reserved a corner of their family room for pots, pans, bed linens, and everything else that would be necessary for their survival.

One of the neighbor girls, Nona, was my best friend, and every twelve months the green-eyed monster of jealousy appeared so strongly that it nearly broke our friendship. I hated the fact that she was vacationing, and I knew in my heart I never would. Every word she spoke about the summers' activities made my envy worse. I also dreaded those two weeks because small-town USA was boring enough with your best friend to share the time with, but without her, it became unbearable.

One summer was different, though. We had an aunt and uncle who had a summer cottage in Lake Delavan, and they invited our family up for a weekend. I was elated. Finally, I too would be able to plan for and then later talk about my adventures in Wisconsin.

The spring days passed at a snail's pace as the anticipation of summer and adventure grew nearer. At last, school was out for the summer, and we would be leaving on the same Saturday as all the neighbors. I would be so proud as we pulled out of our driveway and waved good-bye to them as they still packed their cars.

The day before we were to leave, Mom made my appointment for a physical I needed for kindergarten. Mom never procrastinated, so she thought now would be good to get this physical done, even though two months existed before the fall classes started. Little did I know the physical included a vaccination, which would leave a scab and a permanent mark on my arm. This scab had to fall off naturally, and the doctor gave me orders that I may not, under any circumstances, get it wet. How was I to go swimming in Lake Delavan without getting my arm wet? The vacation was ruined before it even started, but in my mind I was determined to make the best of my dream.

We arrived at the lake in the middle of a downpour of rain and hail. The adults sat by the kitchen table and talked, but there was little for my sisters and me to do except stare out the window, wondering when the rain would stop.

By the next morning, the storm front had passed, and the hot sun was beaming down, causing the blue lake to shimmer. A slight breeze sent tiny ripples across the water as if to say, "Come join the fun." We all changed into our bathing suits and bolted toward the beach, experiencing the sensational warmth of the sand between our toes. Just as I was about to jump into the water, I heard Mom's voice reminding me, "You can't get your arm wet. Don't get in that water!"

I pleaded with Mom; I would only get it a little wet and only once; then it would dry instantly in the heat. Mom never broke the rules and wouldn't ever entertain the idea of disobeying the doctor, so I was forced to sit on the boat dock and just put my feet in the water.

Several years later, I had another chance at a vacation. Vicki's asthma had been terrible that season, and she ended up in the hospital with pneumonia. Her doctor recommended to Mom that she needed to get away for a week to a drier climate so she could recuperate. Mom and Dad discussed it and decided we should fly to Albuquerque, New Mexico, for a week.

At the time, Linda was working for the airlines, so Mom and Dad got free travel. It would only cost for Vicki and me. A year earlier they had traveled to Hawaii with Linda, so they were confident they could master the air travel.

Looking out the window of the airplane on my first flight ever was an awe-inspiring experience. The mountains and rivers below appeared like specks on an endless landscape of brown and green. As the plane climbed effortlessly higher and higher, we were suddenly surrounded by a sea of soft, billowy clouds. *This must be what heaven is like*, I thought to myself. Finally, I would have a real vacation. After the short flight, our plane landed without trauma at the Albuquerque, New Mexico, airport.

As the passengers walked across the tarmac, we felt strong winds pushing us forward. My family went into the airport and gathered our baggage. Next, we needed to secure a shuttle to our motel. We gingerly proceeded to the door, carefully reading every sign that might possibly lead us to our destination. Finally, we arrived at the right spot and boarded our ride.

As the shuttle moved along, we surveyed the landscape. Desert, cactus, and palm trees dotted the sandy but otherwise barren land. As we progressed further, we noticed the winds swirling, causing dust and tumbleweeds to blow across the road in front of us. What an adventure we were about to undertake. It appeared like a scene out of a John Wayne western, except we were not wearing our dusters and bandanas across our face to shield us. I closed my eyes and imagined being on a painted mare, riding along, unafraid of any danger that might befall me from banditos hidden behind the next cactus grove. I was snapped back to reality by Mom's voice saying we would get to our air-conditioned motel, unpack, and give Vicki a chance to relax in the event that the plane ride had been hard for her.

When we arrived at our motel, it was in an area that had little nearby. A restaurant or two were within a short walking distance, and one small store containing necessities and souvenirs was within view. Vicki and I hurriedly unpacked and changed into clothes that seemed more suitable for this arid climate. Mom decided it would be acceptable for all of us to walk to the store and get some rations for our room in order to save on food bills at the restaurants. Twinkies, chips, soda, bread, crackers, and peanut butter were purchased as staples for our trip, along with some candy for a special treat. As we sauntered leisurely back to our room, Vicki's breathing was worse. All the wind and dust was making it difficult for her. We got to the room, and Mom decided we would just stay in the rest of the afternoon and evening to watch the local news, followed by *Gunsmoke* and *Bonanza*, before retiring early.

The local forecast called for high winds with unseasonably high temperatures and humidity. There was an advisory for people with lung conditions to stay indoors in the air as much as possible. Mom was nervous as she listened to report after report. I was not concerned; after all, in Chicago, if the meteorologist called for rain, it would snow; a forecast of heat caused a cold front to move in. By morning surely we would have cooler temperatures with no winds, Vicki's breathing would be better, and Mom and Dad would be so appreciative that their hard-earned money had been invested wisely on this vacation.

After three days of being locked in the motel, we changed our flight, canceled the rest of the week, and flew back to Chicago.

Vicki

Vacations—we never really had one. We were not poor but thrifty. My mother kept house for our neighbors when their family went to Rhinelander, Wisconsin, every year. The good thing about this was that while Mom was cleaning house, we would help, and she allowed us to read their comics. They had every comic that was to be had. What a summer it was! A few times, our parents took us to Lake Delavan, but we barely touched the water because Mom was afraid of the water. We weren't taught how to swim, but we had a wonderful picnic and fun in the sun.

I almost forgot about our vacation to Albuquerque, New Mexico. I had another bad bout with my asthma, just having been released from a hospital stay. My doctor had told my parents we should move to a drier climate. My parents were so loving and always so concerned about my health that they decided to take our family to New Mexico to see if I felt any better in the dry climate there. It would be my first plane ride, and I was so excited! I was amazed at the patchwork view of the earth below us and the clouds that looked like cotton candy as our plane flew right through them. I can still recall the sensation in my ears as they filled with air from the high altitudes at which we were flying. I chewed my Juicy Fruit gum a little harder.

I remember very little about the hotel we stayed at or much about Albuquerque as I spent most of my time in the hotel room. We had chosen to visit when they were having the worst dust storm they had ever had. My doctor suggested a dry climate, but I'm sure he didn't mean this! Gazing out the window of our air-conditioned hotel room, I thought of a song from chorus in High School: "Drifting along with the tumbling tumbleweeds." I really just wanted to go home!

Linda

Like my sisters said, we never went on vacations. Once every year we would pack up the car and head for Lake Geneva for a daytrip. We'd pack a lunch and hang out on the beach. One year the beach was covered with locusts! That didn't stop us. We gingerly stepped over and through them to reach the lake. Later we filled a huge jar full of the bugs for Uncle Bill to use as fishing bait.

I really didn't mind not going on vacations with Mom and Dad because I had Helen and Ruth. Helen and Ruth were both married with children. They would bribe me to come to their houses. I'm not sure if they were lonely or needed someone to help entertain their children, or probably a little of both. With them, I was able to see geysers at Yellowstone National Park; Circus World Museum in Baraboo, Wisconsin; and we took numerous trips to the zoo, park, swimming pool, camping, movies, and many other adventures. Thanks to my older sisters, I was able to see the world and spend time with my nieces and nephews who I love and thoroughly enjoy being with.

Ruth

When I was a little girl growing up in Virgil, family vacations were unheard of. I never knew of a family that took one. We certainly never entertained the thought! We spent our summer days playing outside by ourselves or with the many neighborhood kids.

The highlight of our summer was the trips we made to Lake Geneva, Wisconsin. Only a two-and-a-half-hour drive made this a perfect day trip to swim and picnic. We made a big production of this event and usually invited our Aunt Loretta and cousins Mary Lou, Dorothy, Janie, and Jimmy to accompany us.

Eating was a prominent part of our family dynamics. We weren't fat little girls, only fluffy! For this adventure, we packed lots of picnic foods. We all helped make sandwiches of bologna, lettuce, and butter, or liver sausage, or marshmallow fluff, or even peanut butter and strawberry jelly. Each sandwich was labeled with our individual names because we were all picky about what we would eat. Mom always baked homemade cupcakes, brownies, or cookies. We had chips, Kool-Aid, and a vegetable, like carrots or celery, which was always the last thing to be eaten since we all loved sweets.

Just one highway ran through Lake Geneva with the lake on one side and a big picnic grove on the other where you also parked your cars. As soon as we arrived at the lake, we claimed our spot for the day. We unpacked our food onto a picnic table and spread out our blankets. We then devoured our lunch as if we hadn't eaten in days.

Immediately after eating, we'd beg to get into the water and begin our afternoon of swimming. Mom always made us wait for a full hour before entering the lake. She was determined that we not get stomach cramps and drown, which she felt was a strong possibility. Going in even a few minutes too soon would bring this calamity upon us.

Finally, the hour passed. All suited up, lathered down with suntan lotion, and wearing rubber swimming caps, we crossed the road and entered the clear blue water.

The littlest sisters could only wade out up to their knees, while Helen and I were allowed to go all the way to our waists. None of us could swim, and in those days, no one wore life jackets..

We were five little, fluffy, greased up, snow-white girls in rubber swimming caps wading around in that enormous lake only up to our knees or waists. This was a humorous sight for all the locals who swam with regularity and had bronzed bodies, but we were unaware of their glances. Mom's restrictions did not hamper our fun one bit, and we always had a delightful day.

Early in the evening, we'd pack up our belongings and start our trek home. Our car did not have air conditioning, so it was always hot as we crammed into the backseat. We sisters were worn out and cranky from our day of activities. Without fail, some sister would get her sweaty arm or some other sticky body part against another sister. The bickering and complaining would instantly start. Mom could immediately settle us down, and before we even crossed the Wisconsin border into Illinois, we'd be fast asleep, dreaming of the next time we'd visit Lake Geneva.

Helen

I don't have much to say about vacations. The only time I remember the family talking about trips was when a couple went on a honeymoon. To me, a vacation was just having time off from school, a time to sleep late, a time to read fun books, and a time to play.

A Tale of Five Sisters

My dad worked seven days a week—yes, even on Sundays. Consequently, any car trips were orchestrated by Mom, and she was the driver. The summer tradition that we always looked forward to was the annual day in Lake Geneva, Wisconsin. Mom would pack up us girls and drive for what I thought was at least a thousand miles. We spent our time picnicking and frolicking in the sand and water. At the end of the day, we were all absolutely exhausted and horribly sunburned. We didn't know about skin cancer. It was a memorable, good time.

Any sort of long trip was a rare occasion. My cousin Margie, who lived in Indianapolis, Indiana, was the first of all the cousins to get married. This was one of those occasions. My dad drove, and he wasn't used to navigating in a large city. It was an adventure, especially when, at one point, we found ourselves going the wrong direction on a one-way street. Yikes! I think it was much safer to stay in Virgil where the cars were able to go any direction.

Leaving Virgil

Anita

When I attended high school, there was no push toward college as there is now. Some of my peers would go on to higher education, but many would find a job locally or go into the family farming business. I enjoyed learning and wanted to go for some additional schooling, and I also wanted to leave Virgil to see other places. During my third year, I enrolled in a vocational course for medical office workers. I was interested in helping people, but I knew I was not talented enough, nor did I have the financial wherewithal to go to nursing school. The vocational program was two hours a day during both my junior and senior years and culminated by spending a six-week afternoon internship in a doctor's office.

I excelled in the program, earning all A's the entire time. My internship was with a doctor in Batavia who specialized in prescribing diet pills to his obese female clients. While this experience was not particularly rewarding, I did realize that it was what I wanted to do after school. My teacher told me that I might want to consider going to a junior college and getting a medical office assistant certification. The certification would give me some extra skills and also a higher starting wage. This seemed like the perfect solution—I could pursue an interesting career and also attend college. To make the situation even more inviting, the only college that offered such a program was Belleville Area College in downstate Belleville, Illinois. I would be able to pay in-district tuition through our local community college but still move away from Virgil.

My best friend and neighbor, Nona, was so envious. She had graduated from school a year earlier than I did and was living at home, working as a hostess at a local restaurant. Although she did like her job, she felt trapped. The perfect solution came to us. Why not move to Belleville with me, share an apartment, and get a job there? Together we would have adventures. I applied to Belleville Area College and received my acceptance letter, pending academic testing in spring on campus in Belleville.

On a muggy, humid April day, my mother, Nona, and I checked into a local family-owned motel nestled at the edge of Main Street, close to the school campus. After putting our bags in the room, we set out to see what Belleville had to offer. Belleville is the St. Clair County Seat, so there was a huge court and judicial complex that stood at the center of town. As we approached, it appeared to us that the stately courthouse, built in the late 1800s, was looming over the town square, keeping a watchful eye on the traffic and the people as they bustled in and out of the buildings doing their all-important, probably life-altering activities.

Our next stop was the Cathedral of St. Peter, the home of the Catholic Diocese of Belleville. This is where we would be attending Mass on Sunday mornings, we promised Mom. Reading the literature in the rectory, we learned that the archbishop himself held the 9:00 a.m. Mass on Sunday. We were in awe. This would be the closest to God that we had ever come.

Proceeding on, we found the usual fast-food restaurants, some Mom and Pop diners and stores, and, of course, the Fairview Heights Mall. Feeling a bit hungry and overwhelmed by all the grandeur, we stopped for a bite to eat at the local Denny's restaurant, which later would become Nona's employer and our late-night haven.

The next morning, we arose early, still giddy from yesterday's adventure. As I opened the blinds to the parking lot, we saw a small group of soldiers wearing brown camouflaged clothing. They stood near some Jeeps, conversing with several men dressed in dark blue suits, decked out with medals and bars on the sleeves. Another exciting discovery! Scott Air Force Base was located outside of town. Many of the weekend warriors stayed at this motel the night before they had to report. Nona and I had never seen a military man this close. We had only seen pictures of my uncle John in his WWII war pictures as they sat on the mantel at Grandma's house. We knew we would be safe in Belleville with the military and the Catholic Church watching over us.

At 8:45, I proceeded to drive to the school, leaving Mom and Nona at the room to read a book, work crossword puzzles, or watch TV. As I drove, I felt butterflies in my stomach—no, worse than that, giant killer moths fighting within me.

I arrived at the huge campus and followed the signs to the testing site. Knowing that my and Nona's whole future rested on my passing the placement test, I said a quick prayer and forced myself to enter the building. Much to my delight, the testing was over in two hours. I had passed with points to spare, and I would be allowed to enroll in classes when I got my official letter.

I drove back to the motel, giddy, excited, and scared. Soon, Belleville, Illinois, would be my new home. Tears, hugs, and laughter met me as I told Nona I had passed the tests. Mom also hugged me, and a tear formed at the corner of her eyes. She said she was proud that her daughter would be a college student, but years later she told me how upset she was that I would be leaving home. I was the youngest. Many years later, when my youngest, Rebecca, went off to college, Mom confided in me how hard it was for her when I left. The house was suddenly empty and quiet and so big for just her and Dad. Every time she heard a rattle at the backdoor, she thought it was me coming home from school.

The next months became a blur. Finals at school, graduation, packing, and selecting classes made the days peel off the calendar quickly. Finally, it was the Fourth of July weekend. Nona and I were going to drive Dad's 1968 steel-blue Nova because he and Mom had decided to allow us to keep it. Nona's parents and little sister were going to follow us in their vehicle and stay at a motel that weekend to help us get set up. Mom and Dad would come down in two weeks and bring anything else we needed. Both cars were filled to the max with all of our personal possessions that would be essential in our new life.

Hugs and kisses to Mom and Dad, and we were off. Inside, I was petrified at that moment. What had I done? Why did I want to leave my home and the people I loved to move to a large town filled with strangers? This was my decision, and I could not turn back now. I put the car in reverse and pulled out of the driveway, not letting the fear overtake my body.

Aunt Mary knew a woman in Belleville, probably a distant cousin twice removed, but still family. This woman had found us an apartment to rent at 1923 Avenue B, Apt. 201, Belleville, Illinois. It would be our new address. According to the AD we received, it was a two-bedroom, with kitchen, bath, and a shower, renting for only 100 dollars a month, and furnished. It was affordable, even on our meager budget. My dad had already retired, so I received a small Social Security payment each month, and Nona would get a job. Mom promised to send me the Sunday church bulletin and a ten-dollar bill each week so I could keep up on the local news and have a little mad money. My schooling was paid for by an Illinois state grant, so I did not have to worry about that either.

We pulled into the pothole-filled, six-space parking area in the alley of our new home. The building itself was a run-down, six-apartment dwelling with a drab olive-green shingled roof and a weathered exterior of gray chipping paint. We accessed our second floor apartment by a set of stairs leading to an outer porch adjoining three apartments. A bit apprehensive, we climbed the stairs and turned the key to the apartment. It was probably beautiful on the inside, we thought to ourselves; after all, it had been family that found this place for us.

The early afternoon sun came streaming in the large window overlooking the kitchen sink. This was a good thing because the kitchen light did not work, and without the sunlight, we might not have seen how filthy the sink looked. Some Comet cleanser and some Mr. Clean on the dirty floor tiles, and it would be livable.

The next room we surveyed was the living room. The sagging couch in the corner would need a throw cover, but it would be usable. The two chairs were serviceable, and the seventeen-inch color television that was in my car would fit nicely on the end table that sat near the chairs.

The bedrooms needed some tender-loving care, more Mr. Clean, some bright curtains, and our favorite bedding on the beds, and then it would be more attractive.

Last room was the bathroom. Oh, what a sight the rust-laden toilet and bathtub were. The advertised shower consisted of an extension pipe affixed to the back of the old cast-iron tub, running upward about three feet. The contraption leaned forward due to the weight of the calcium-covered showerhead. Also, attached at the top of the pipe was a round halo covering the tub for a shower curtain.

Nona and I would have sat down and wept except we were afraid to touch anything. Nona's mom sprung into action. A girl raised on the farm, she was accustomed to hard work and knew that, with a trip to the hardware store for supplies, we could fix this mess.

"Make a list, girls," she barked out. "We need Mr. Clean, scrub buckets, rags, window cleaner, a shower faucet, toilet seat, and curtains." On and on the list went until, as writer's cramp set in my right hand, she finally stopped.

Nona's parents had generously offered to pay for this trip to the store. It was not in our meager budget at this time, and they understood. It would be their housewarming gift to us. After emptying our belongings out of their car and into our new home, we proceeded to the store, where we filled the shopping cart with all the items on the list.

We arrived back at the apartment and began our chores. Nona's mom had the plan all laid out. She had the bathroom, I had the kitchen, Nona and her little sis had the living room, and Nona's dad would do all the handiwork needed. After that, we would all work on the bedrooms.

At about 9:00, with the place looking livable, it was time for Nona's parents to go to their motel. Already homesick and somewhat afraid to stay alone, we convinced Nona's little sister to spend the night with us. We all three sat down on the couch and turned on the TV. It was Friday night, and we had decided to stay up late for the 10:30 movie. We were past exhausted but too nervous to sleep.

Just as the evening news anchor appeared on the screen, we heard a loud crash coming from the apartment next door. A booming male voice spewed out profanities, which were answered with sobs and crying from a female voice. Panic-stricken, the three of us huddled together, trying to shield our ears from the noise. Didn't this barbarian realize that nobody should ever raise their voice to a lady? We sat motionless a while longer, trying to decide what to do. We wanted to run out of the apartment, down the steps, and to the safety of the motel room of Nona's parents, but we were afraid. What if the voice came out of the apartment next door and started to speak to us?

After what seemed like an eternity, but in reality it was probably only fifteen minutes, it quieted next door. We turned down the TV and turned off all the lights except for one small one in the corner. We would watch the movie and try to forget what we just heard.

Moments after the lights were lowered, we sensed something moving across the floor. Maybe it was a small spider, bug, or even a fly. We had been raised in the country, so this did not scare us. After a few more moments, there seemed to be a whole community assembling. I snapped on a light, and we saw these multi-legged creatures with radar-like antennae scurrying back into the darkness from which they had come. That was it. We had to get out of this trap! We would risk our life passing the man's house because we would never stay here with these silver-backed bugs that we had never before seen in our lives. We grabbed our purses and bolted out of the apartment, breathless as we arrived unharmed to our car.

We drove the few miles to the safety of the parents' motel, where we slept on the floor the rest of the night.

The next morning, my roommate and I made the decision to never again step foot in that place. Her parents had to go back alone and retrieve our possessions. They then helped us find a more suitable residence that we could live in so that we would not have to return to Virgil, defeated by the cockroaches and the inebriated neighbor.

Vicki

After my graduation from Kaneland High School, it was just assumed that I would find a job and live at home until whenever. I did find a job at the Portable Tool Factory in Geneva, located approximately forty-five minutes from home.

My mustard-colored Ford Maverick—named Mergie—and I would make the trek Monday through Friday each week. I was so excited! I would be making $3.60 an hour at my first full-time job. The job entailed working on an assembly line, making radial arm saws. I became good at it and made many good friends in spite of my shyness.

I worked with Hispanic people. I had never met one before, as Virgil consisted of only German Caucasians. These workers sang constantly and were happy people. I was captivated. I could not understand their language, but we became friends. I also met the most intriguing man who was blind. It was amazing how he worked. I found out he was also a DJ for a local radio station. We became great friends, and he taught me how to crack my chewing gum. I began to realize what a sheltered life I had led and how much I was beginning to learn about this whole new world.

It was at Portable Tool that I met my first husband, Al. I became immediately smitten by him, as he was the first man to ever pay any attention to me. He had dark, thick hair; large brown eyes; and he adored me. What more could I want? Yes, he had no money, could not hold down a job, played too much pool, and had a drinking problem, but I was in love with him. Yeah, sometimes I had to pay his rent for him, but I knew that things would get better. He just didn't come from a family like mine. His father abandoned him at the age of five. His mother married five times. I knew if he had someone who loved and supported him, he would change. He just needed a little help getting started.

At the age of twenty-one, we were married, and I moved out of the house to a small apartment in Geneva. It was a hard life, but I knew if I loved him enough, I could change these habits of his and we would live happily ever after. Seems I had brought my rose-colored glasses from Virgil with me.

Unfortunately, all the love in the world could not change him, but we had two beautiful children together before we separated after seven years of marriage filled with many struggles.

Still, through all this, my parents remained supportive. I knew they constantly worried about me, but they were never judgmental. I look back at this time of my life and am amazed at the way they handled this situation. They were the wisest people I have ever known.

I have taken these years of my life and learned from them.

- I have learned I cannot change people. Another person's life is their own. They are responsible for their own decisions, and no other person has control over them. Influence, yes—control, no.

- Al was an alcoholic, and alcoholism is a disease. The only thing that really matters to an alcoholic is alcohol. An alcoholic will remain an alcoholic for the rest of his/her life. If an alcoholic wants to live a normal life, they must realize they have a problem. They must seek support from family and support groups. They should call upon God for His help.

- I have learned I am an enabler. Maybe you figured that out when I spoke about Al's family history. I was great at making excuses for him. Having learned this about myself, I can try not to fall into this habit again. Enabling is more harmful than it is helpful, even though it is done out of love—so is discipline and setting boundaries.

- I don't fault only Al for the failure of our marriage. It was also my naivety. I was a small-town girl getting her first look at life in the big cities—meaning anywhere with a population over 200 people. At the age of nineteen, I hadn't experienced enough in life to even know who I was or what I wanted.

- I became a single mom raising her two children. I put my faith in God and asked for His help. Money was tight, but I managed. We had all we needed. I had a job. We had food, housing, and love.

- Family—what this book is really all about. I knew my family was always there for me. My parents had taught me the importance of family, and I would raise mine with the same ideals.

- Blessings—Valerie and Chris Foley. Out of this failed marriage, I took with me these two children who were gifts from God. I would never stop providing for them and loving them.

Our lives don't always play out the way we think they should or even how our parents think they should, but God has a special plan for each and every one of us. With God's help, we can use every situation, whether good or bad, and learn from it. Hint, hint—I did much better in my second marriage.

Linda

After high school graduation, Mom and Dad expected me to get a job. Up until then, I just did babysitting. My older sisters had jobs when they were in high school and that caused a lot of work and extra driving around for Mom, so I was not allowed to get a job.

My first job was at a factory, welding lead wires on tubes that were used for electronics. I hated that job and came home crying to Mom and Dad about it. They said before I was allowed to quit, I had to find another job. Next, I got a job at UPS, but I still wanted more.

I decided I wanted to work for the airlines. I took a correspondence course with Weaver Airline School and left home for the first time to complete the school with one month of classroom training in Kansas City. I received my Certificate of Completion and was hired by United Airlines.

A short time later, I got an apartment in Mount Prospect. It was there at that apartment I met a strikingly handsome young sailor named Jim. He later became my soul mate and husband. Six months after our wedding, Jim got orders to go to Guam, and I was allowed to accompany him.

It was extremely difficult leaving my family. Mom and I cried so hard when we had to say good-bye, because we knew we would not see each other for two years. Mom faithfully wrote letters, and my sisters kept me informed of the daily happenings.

What a joyous reunion we had when Jim and I returned from our overseas assignment. We were delighted to introduce our new baby boy, Benjamin, to his grandparents, aunts, uncles, and cousins.

Through all of our adventures, we came to the conclusion that there's no place like *Virgil!*

Ruth

Although our parents never mentioned the subject, we girls knew that after graduation we were expected to leave home and begin our adult lives. This was a scary time but also an exciting one.

Immediately after graduation from high school, Helen and a friend from school got their first apartment. Helen worked for an insurance agency in St. Charles and later secured a job at the phone company in Geneva.

The day Helen left home was the best day of my life. It meant I'd get to take possession of her much-coveted bedroom. After fourteen years of sharing one bedroom with my three little sisters, I was elated to finally have a bedroom entirely to myself. I wasted no time moving in, and within a few days, I made that room my own with magazine posters plastered everywhere. My floor, from wall to wall, was strewn knee-deep with clothes. Ah, so cozy!

I was in heaven, except for one problem, I was afraid to sleep alone! I needed to entice one of my little sisters to sleep with me. Linda demanded a quarter every night. Vicki had respiratory problems and needed to be checked by Mom every night. And Anita regularly wet the bed. My choice, naturally, was Linda, even though she was a little pricey.

On nights when my sisters could not be coerced to sleep in my room, I kept a butcher knife under my pillow. Finally, I got used to my room and fell asleep to radio music. My dad would come in early in the morning and turn the radio off, never complaining, even though he regularly instructed me to turn the music off before I got too sleepy. Our parents were sympathetic and extremely patient with us.

When it came my time to graduate from high school, I had no idea what I would do. I didn't want to go on to college like many of my friends. Maybe I'd be a missionary or an English teacher. In actuality, I became a waitress! What I really wanted to do was get married.

I had a crazy, tumultuous romance with John Kenyon throughout my high school years. We either loved or hated each other. My parents put up with so much from us: all the nights I cried myself to sleep, Mom waiting up for me to come home in the wee morning hours, or John banging on our door in the middle of the night to talk to me. I remember those cold winter nights when John was living in his car and sleeping in our driveway. Dad would go out and invite him in to sleep on our couch so, as Dad put it, "he wouldn't freeze to death."

Once, after an unusually bad break-up causing my sister Vicki to kneel and pray the rosary outside of my bedroom door, I packed up every gift that John had ever given me. I dramatically returned the huge stack of treasures and trinkets to him, including a record player with a large collection of 45s; a beautiful, natural fur coat; a mountain of stuffed animals; and lots of other goodies. John promptly took all these items out to our driveway and built a big bonfire with them. My Mom, who had the patience of Job, went outside and said, "John, don't you think you have made that fire a little too close to our house?"

We had so many fights and also so many exciting and awesome adventures that we must have driven Mom and Dad half crazy.

In February of 1963, I finally did leave home, but not to get married. John and I had already secretly been married two weeks earlier. One evening, at midnight, right after my shift at the diner, we were married by a justice of the peace. I wore my white waitress uniform, and John wore a red ski sweater.

After the ceremony, John took me back home because we were afraid to tell my parents what we had done. One evening Dad found us downstairs on the couch in a compromising situation, and John had to tell him about our marriage.

It was a difficult time for Mom and Dad because we had married outside of the Catholic Church. In our community, this was a huge disgrace for our family. That night, after I packed my things and left home, I looked back, and Mom was crying.

Helen

It was a customary rite of passage that when you graduated from high school, you would naturally leave home. After my short stint in college, I got a job working for the telephone office in Geneva, Illinois. I was one of those operators who would say, "Number please," when you picked up your phone. That was long before cell phones; I've seen a lot of changes in technology.

Geneva was at least thirty miles from Virgil, so I teamed up with a girlfriend, and we rented an apartment. That was a real learning experience. Much to my chagrin, I found out other people had very different styles of living. My so-called friend was not a steady worker; she was prone to party hard at night and not go to work the next day. She often invited friends to the apartment while I was at work. They felt at liberty to use our facilities and borrow my clothes. Laying hands on my clothes was the catalyst that broke up the friendship and prompted me to get a room in the home of an elderly couple.

That couple, Paul and Vi Boles, treated me like a daughter, but I spent very little time there, mostly just to sleep because I worked at the telephone company during the days of the week, and I continued to work at Rex's Drive-In as a carhop on the weekends. I always had money to buy clothes from my favorite dress store, the Merri-Lee Shop. That shop is still in existence in the same spot on the corner of Third and State in Geneva.

When I first started working at the drive-in several years before, the proprietor, Rex, jokingly told me that if I played my cards right, I would probably have the opportunity to meet a millionaire. Well, that didn't happen. When you're an immature, self-centered young woman, you look for other qualities. So naturally I fell madly in love with a cute guy in a snazzy car who tipped big and persistently asked me to date him. That would have been my future husband, Gordon.

Good-bye, Dad, We Still Miss You

Anita

*I*t was a glorious Sunday morning in April of 1979. The daffodils and tulips were in full bloom, and all the trees were starting to bud. Even though it was only 9:00 a.m., the sun was smiling down on all of this activity, proud of its work in progress. My husband, Jackie, and I were driving out to Virgil to have an early Easter lunch with the family. Linda, Vicki, and I had commitments for the next weekend, which was actually Easter, so Mom made plans to serve us a week earlier. As my husband drove from our apartment in Aurora, I was daydreaming about the meal, almost tasting the sweetness of the honey-glazed ham, feeling the few lumps of the homemade mashed potatoes across my tongue, and trying to map out my plan for saving room for the crowning glory of Mom's meal, her homemade lemon meringue and pumpkin pie.

We turned the corner onto IC Trail Road, and
I could see an ambulance in the driveway of our
house. I had talked to Mom not an hour before, and
everything was fine, so I could not imagine what this
was about. As we pulled into the drive, I jumped out
of the car and raced into the house to see what was
happening. Mom stood in the doorway between the
dining room and the living room. She was in tears but
as composed as she always was. I looked past her and
saw a paramedic beating on the chest of a lifeless figure
that was sprawled across my dad's favorite resting
place, the old green couch.

Mom came alongside me and explained in a voice
barely audible that Dad was having a heart attack.
After helping her peel potatoes, Dad had lain down for
a nap while Mom prepared the rest of the meal. She
could hear the rumbling of his snoring as she happily
bustled around the kitchen, attending to every little
detail of the meal. Suddenly, his snoring stopped, and
she heard a large gasp, followed by nothing. She ran to
his side and shook him, but there was no response. She
then frantically called the EMTs who arrived about
ten minutes later.

Just as she finished telling me the events, the phone
rang. It was the neighbors calling to see what was going
on. Mom told me to answer and tell them that Dad
was having trouble and then to call my sisters—Linda
and Vicki—and try to get them before they came for
lunch. Mom did not want them witnessing what was
happening and to get hysterical; we needed to stay
calm and let the EMTs take care of the situation, she

reasoned with me. Dutifully, I did as she requested, lying to my brother-in-law Jim about the gravity of the situation when he answered the phone. Thank goodness they were always late and they had not left their home. After promising to call them as soon as Dad was stabilized, I hung up and dialed Vicki. She must have been on the way with her husband and their baby, Valerie, because the phone just rang and rang.

Minutes that seemed like an eternity passed, and still the ambulance crew worked. They now had the paddles out and were trying to shock Dad's heart back into a rhythm. *Come on, Dad, don't die*, I thought to myself. CPR resumed, then another round of the shock, and still no motion from the couch.

Finally, the leader of the crew looked at Mom and spoke the cruelest words that I had ever heard: "I am sorry, but he is gone. We tried everything we could."

In disbelief, I deliberated on what kind of mean joke was being played on my family. We were here for dinner to celebrate the resurrection of Christ from the tomb, not to watch Dad die.

As I started to sob, Mom came over and put her arms around me and told me we needed to be strong. Vicki had arrived moments earlier and was bewildered about what was unfolding in front of her. She needed to be informed, and then we needed to call back Linda and tell her family, and then the neighbors and the other sisters and all the relatives.

Knowing that I needed to be strong, I put on my best game face and proceeded to approach the tasks ahead with a detached, business-like demeanor. There would be plenty of time later for mourning, but right now Mom expected me to be in charge. Stoically, she and I made all the necessary phone calls, and after several hours, we sat down to let it all sink in. In the blink of an eye, our lives were forever changed. We had all been planning this Easter celebration of joy, but now it was one of sadness and deep pain.

The next three days were a blur of obligatory activities. All the sisters and their spouses arrived at the house, and together we had to go to the funeral home to make final arrangements. It was a surreal experience that I had to detach myself from in order to remain calm. We were escorted into the basement of the local funeral home. Displayed as artwork were caskets, vaults, and pictures of flower arrangements from which we could make our selections. Price ranges were neatly attached to each piece so we could plan what was most affordable for our budget.

"Mahogany and cherry wood are more expensive than walnut, but they all look regal with gold handles attached," the director explained. Most men preferred off-white satin lining over pure white, but, of course, it was our decision. The funeral director droned on and on. I wanted to remind him that we were not redecorating a sitting parlor, but I knew this was all part of the ritual of passage from this world to the next and provided a sense of peace and closure to many.

With this chore behind us, we still had to overcome the next hurdle: a wake and funeral service. Vicki and I were both pregnant at the time, and both of us fainted at the wake as we saw Dad lying peacefully in the casket surrounded by flowers, the words of the priest echoing, "Eternal rest grant unto his soul." It was final. Once that casket top slammed, we would never see our father again.

The only peace and joy was in listening to the many stories that everyone shared. According to family history, Dad was one of ten children born to German immigrant parents. The farm that was purchased in Virgil was a way for the family to survive. They tended to crops and raised livestock for their own consumption and to sell at market. Because of their German descent, consumption of beer was an acceptable practice, but Dad and several of his brothers dealt with the demon of alcoholism most of their lives. According to one uncle, unlike many drinkers, Dad was always a gentle and fun-loving man who did not turn mean and spiteful when inebriated. He enjoyed after-work social hour at the local Virgil tavern, often getting involved in card games that lasted till Mom would appear to bring him home hours later. But it was noted that he never missed work and loved his wife and daughters passionately. Other stories were shared about how skilled Dad was in the use of dynamite, so whenever someone needed a tree stump removed on their farms, Dad was always the man to call. He was a respected member of the community and would be missed by all.

Many of the stories that were shared about Dad and the things he did while under the influence were foreign to me, as if they were talking about a total stranger. I did not know any of this history personally because Dad practiced abstinence for as long as I could remember.

Dad retired from the Modern Dairy Milk Company when I was young. I remember Mom and him getting dressed up one Friday evening for his retirement party. Mom had on a gorgeous sapphire blue dress that she had purchased in a store, not sewn herself—as was the practice with most of our clothing. She had on high heel shoes and bright red lipstick. Dad had on his best suit that was reserved for weddings and funerals, so I knew that this was indeed a momentous occasion.

After that evening, Dad never again got up and left in his red Chevy pickup for the long drive to Elgin. Instead, every morning, he could be found sitting at the kitchen table drinking his instant Hills Brothers Coffee, complete with milk and a teaspoon of sugar. He would say good morning but rarely utter another word. He was seemingly content to just being an observer in the activities as they unfolded around him.

After the morning rush of everybody getting ready to catch the school bus, he would retreat to his basement workshop where he, as Mom called it, "tinkered around" till we all arrived home after our day's activities. At the supper table, he would again sit silently listening with intense interest as his girls chattered on about their day. When the supper table was cleared and the dishwashing duties started, Dad would withdraw to his favorite chair in the living room. Out of the earshot of the inevitable bickering that would ensue between his children, he read the evening paper and watched his favorite shows, including *Gunsmoke, Bonanza,* and *The Rifleman.*

Rarely did Dad get involved with discipline unless Mom sent one of us to him because we were out of line. When we crossed that invisible line, wearing her patience to a frazzle, Mom would say, "Go tell your Dad what you did!" Without any further discussion, we would go confess to our father what had happened. He listened carefully as we gave our most compelling plea for leniency, but the sentence was always the same regardless of how heinous or innocent the crime.

"Your Mom loves you and does her best, go and tell her you are sorry," came his judgment. How I hated those words. Just once I hoped that he would agree with me and realize that Mom was wrong, but it never happened. Grudgingly, I always did as Dad said because he was in charge and I had the deepest love and respect for him.

To this day, I still miss my dad. I wish that my daughters had grown up with him in their lives, and I wish for myself that I had the opportunity to sit with him in that kitchen in Virgil and sip coffee and learn how, through silence, to communicate.

Vicki

Dad was the first person I had ever seen die. As Al, Valerie, and I approached our home in Virgil for that Sunday meal, I was shocked to see an ambulance with its lights flashing in our front yard. As we entered the house, I saw dad lying on his favorite green couch.

Standing over him were paramedics administering CPR. I kept thinking, *No, Dad, no. You'll never get to meet your grandson, and your granddaughter isn't even three yet. We all still need you.* But it was God's time to take my dad home to be with him.

The next days were a blur of sadness and memories. My dad was a kind, soft-spoken, caring man. He was a quiet man; he never gossiped and only spoke when he had something to say of importance. He was a loving father, and I would miss him dearly.

Even though Dad left for work early and had long hours, he always seemed to have time for us. I remember he would lie on his back on the floor, feet in the air. We would sit or lay across his feet, and he would balance us. Even though I was an awkward girl, I felt like an accomplished acrobat with Dad's help. Also, I remember dancing with my dad. This was during the time of 45 rpm and 78 rpm records. We had one called "Eating Goober Peas." Dad had a dance routine that he would perform with us. Not exactly *Dancing with the Stars* material, but we thought we were good.

I had a terrible temper as a child. I remember sitting on my dad's lap as he gently talked to me about my temper. He never had to spank me. I only had to look into his disappointed eyes, and I started to cry. I would like to say this only happened once, but no, it was many times. Each time I felt terrible about not being able to control my temper and how sad it made my dad, but it was all Linda's fault!

I will never forget the Saturday trips with Dad to the bank and Dad's Hardware in Maple Park. I always felt special when I would be chosen to go. The bank always gave you a lollipop, and at Dad's Hardware, my dad would buy me shoestring licorice. It was the longest, thinnest licorice, and you probably could have used it for shoelaces, but it was more fun to tie into knots—making rings and then eating it.

Dad was the one who taught me how to drive, and I was a terrible driver. I remember car shopping with Dad at the auto dealership in Sycamore. That was where our family bought all of our cars. I saw a baby-blue Volkswagen that I really liked; however, it was a stick shift, and I only knew how to drive an automatic. The dealership told us to take the car home for a week and see if I could drive it. Dad, being the patient man that he was, would take me out in the VW to teach me how to drive.

One day, as I was driving on a country road, I saw red flashing lights in my rearview mirror. It was a police officer, and he was pulling me over. I turned to Dad, and he said, "Just pull over. It'll be okay." The officer asked for my license and inquired about the car. It didn't have any plates on it, so he assumed it was stolen. After we were back on our way again, I turned to Dad and said, "If I wanted to steal a car, I certainly would have stolen one that I could drive!" This became a joke between the two of us, and soon we returned the VW and I got my mustard-colored Maverick.

After dad retired from the dairy, he was still active fixing things around the house. He was used to getting up early from working at the dairy, and it was not uncommon when we got up in the morning to find dad wandering around with a hammer or tool in his hand, still clad in his pajamas. I will never forget Dad's inventions. We lived in a very old house with a bathroom with sink, toilet, and tub in the upper story. Dad set up a shower in the basement that consisted of a pipe with a watering can sprinkler head attached to it. This was an ingenious shower that we were all excited to have. He also made a wiener roaster by using 220 current that pulsed through the wiener on a post. It was a quick, delicious, fun meal. Dad was always willing to help with any school projects too.

It has been just over thirty years ago since my dad died, and I still feel his loss. I know I will see him in heaven, and I know he looks down upon me, my children, and my grandchildren. I know he is smiling just as I smile when I remember how great my dad was.

Linda

Saying good-bye to Dad was one of the most difficult things I've had to do!

I remember I was working the day he passed away, and I got a call from my husband, Jim, saying I should come home immediately. I kept asking why, because I couldn't just leave my job for no apparent reason. Jim was apprehensive but finally told me my father had passed away. I felt like someone had just pulled my heart out. I promptly left work and cried and sobbed the whole way home. After arriving home, we packed up the car and the kids and headed out to Virgil to be with family. Dad died so unexpectedly; none of us were prepared for it. Everything after that became a blur. I can only remember not being able to stop crying. For the next couple of months, I would wake up crying. Every time I thought about Dad or if someone would mention him, I would cry. Finally, one night I decided to write about the memories I had of my father. This was a great comfort to me. To my dismay, I cannot locate my story.

My father was a quiet, gentle man. He was a man of few words but was respected by many. He was a very hard worker and could fix just about anything. I used to help him work on projects; my job was to hold the flashlight and get his tools out of his toolbox for him. Dad was always a good sport, being the father of five daughters, he would sit patiently as his hair was being put in rollers or ponytails! When we would go to the carnival, he was always the one who would ride on the scary rides with us. Dad loaned me money for my first car.

After I received my paycheck, we would go together to his desk, and he'd pull the ledger out and write my payment down. Dad taught me financial responsibility. When Dad retired, he got a beagle that he named Max. When we would come home to visit, we would be treated to a performance by Max showing off the few tricks he learned. My mother and father were good examples for us. There was mutual respect and love between them both, and I felt secure and loved. Even though Dad is gone, memories of him will go on forever.

Ruth

Our car was strangely and unusually quiet as we made the eight-hour trip from Camdenton, Missouri, to Virgil, Illinois. My mind was racing. *How could my Dad be dead? It was just a few weeks ago that he and Mom made a trip down to visit us.*

On one of their visits , Dad was driving their brand-new car. We owned a cantankerous goat that was overcome at the sight of that shiny new vehicle parked in our driveway. To my dad's horror, that goat jumped all the way up on the roof of his car. When my husband demanded the goat get off, he reared up and jumped down as hard as he could, all four feet landing on the middle of the hood, where he proceeded to bounce up and down.

On the following morning, as my dad awoke, he was shocked when he looked over and saw his nemesis, the goat, standing right in their bed atop of Mom who was screaming, "George, get this goat off me!" Immediately, Dad rolled over and went back to sleep! No, I'm just kidding. Dad grabbed that crazy goat and shooed him out the door.

Dad also had an unpleasant experience in the woods, where he got into a nest of chiggers and had hundreds of red itchy bites around his tender white city ankles. Dad was gracious about all these incidents.

On another visit, I rented some polka records from our library, and we all danced with sock monkeys until late in the evening. *And now*, I thought to myself, *my dad is gone. I'll never see him again. How can I stand it?*

To some people, my Dad probably looked like any ordinary man. He usually dressed in bibbed overalls with a blue long-sleeved work shirt. His pocket held his Elgin pocket watch attached by a brown shoelace. He also carried a blue or red handkerchief. Under this attire he wore white long johns, even to bed. My Dad wore glasses, and he was nearly bald, except for a fringe of brown hair around his head just like Robin Hood's friend Friar Tuck. Dad had a one-inch scar on his forehead, which was a constant reminder of the time he tried to roller-skate on the ice down at the creek when he was a boy.

My dad was a wonderful person. He was patient, as is evident by the fact that he taught each of his daughters to drive using his stick-shift truck. I remember the day he brought that bright-red Chevy pickup home. He had purchased it without Mom's knowledge or permission. That was one of the few times I ever saw them fight. Mom swore she would never ride in that truck, and I don't know if she ever did!

Mostly, Dad was respectful of Mom. He never disagreed with her and was always supportive. He dutifully gave her his paycheck every week. She was responsible for the family budget and took care of all expenses. She gave him his weekly spending money. He never complained or asked for any more.

Dad probably spent most of his allowance at the little tavern just down the street and across the road from our home. Stopping in for a drink after work was a custom of many of the men in our town. With my dad, as with many of the other men, it never stopped with just one drink. Mom would send Helen or me into the tavern to tell Dad it was time to come home or that supper was waiting. He proudly showed us off to his bar friends, many of whom were our uncles or cousins. We often forgot Mom was waiting as we were often treated to candy bars, soda pop, chips, or—my favorite—dried, smoked herring.

Dad always drank the same combination of 100-proof Old Grand Dad whiskey and a glass of beer. This was called a "Boiler maker." Once, he introduced this drink to my future husband, who then wound up in a snow bank outside of the bar in the middle of the night with his future mother-in-law trying to pull him out. After Mom finally got Dad and John back home, they proceeded to wrestle on my bed, where John broke Dad's glasses and then high-tailed it to the bathroom, where he threw up most of the night. In the morning, Dad, who was all smiles, said, "That John, he's one hundred percent!" Anyone or anything that Dad particularly liked, he called "one hundred percent."

When my dad drank, he both stuttered and staggered—not a pretty sight. In my teen years I was really embarrassed by him, and I readily told him so. I was nasty and sassy to him, but he never seemed to mind, nor did he change his routine for me. If I was having a school friend overnight, I would make him promise not to stop off at the bar but to come straight home after work. He would obediently promise, but it never happened. When my daughter, Carla, was born, an amazing thing occurred. My dad just suddenly stopped drinking! Years later, he told me this story.

One evening, he was sitting in the tavern, enjoying his usual libation. He looked around and said to himself, "I don't want to be like this anymore. God, will you please help me?" He got up off the barstool, walked out the door, and never drank again—except for the shot of whiskey he had every Christmas.

My Dad was a quiet and gentle man. He never raised his voice at us kids. I can't remember ever being spanked, although we were occasionally scolded by him. Mom took care of most of the discipline in our home. If we did something she considered especially wrong, she would wait until Dad came home. We then would have to confess it to him. I would rather have been beaten within an inch of my life than to have to endure the silence that followed my confession. Finally, after what seemed like an eternity, Dad would say something like, "Well, never do that again. Now go help your mother."

Mom called Dad "the boss." If we needed permission to do something or to go somewhere, Mom would say, "Go ask the boss." Now we knew who the real boss was, but we would dutifully make our requests to Dad, who always responded by saying, "Whatever your mom thinks is all right."

My Dad could snore louder than any man I have ever known. He also had the strongest teeth. He never went to the dentist and never had a cavity. We bragged about how he could lift one of us girls in the air while we were seated on a little chair with only his teeth. And remember, we were not lightweights!

Dad had been a mechanic working with Uncle Mike at the filling station in our town. Dad always did his own car repairs and tune-ups. He also maintained each girl's car when we were old enough to drive. This included regularly checking our oil and filling our gas tanks from the barrel he kept at home.

Sharing a one-bathroom house with his wife and five daughters was a bit of a challenge. The basement was Dad's sanctuary. There he kept a plethora of tools and gadgets neatly categorized and arranged. He needed this array of equipment because of all the things he tinkered with. There was a big dump in the next town of Lily Lake, where Dad collected all sorts of gears, metal frames, tires, and odds and ends. He brought these treasures home to make endless inventions and creations. We always had interesting bikes made from someone's discarded scraps.

One of my favorite memories was the time Dad surprised me with a new doll. Dad had found some broken dolls and salvaged enough parts to make a complete baby for me. The only obstacle was that there were no usable legs, so Dad fashioned me a lovely doll using arms to replace the missing legs. I was pretty little then and couldn't pronounce my R's. When Dad showed me that doll, my eyes lit up as I proclaimed, "Oh, my dolly is all aams!" I took it everywhere and was so proud that my dad made it especially for me.

My Dad loved to listen to *The Lone Ranger* on the radio, and later he faithfully watched him on the television.

When my Dad was a boy growing up on the family
farm, one of his chores was to help deliver the spring
calves. Imagine his surprise when he helped to birth
a little two-headed calf. The wee brown calf lived for
several days and was the talk of Virgil. When it passed
away, Dad had it stuffed by a friend who was studying
to be a taxidermist. Dad was really proud of his calf
and kept it for the rest of his life.

We will never forget our wonderful Dad, and the
many memories of his life will live forever in our hearts.

Helen

April 8, 1979, I was living in Geneseo, Illinois, with
my husband, Gordon, and my four children: Gretchen,
Kelly, Vanessa, and Michelle. I remember so clearly what
I was doing, like other important times when something
shocks you—like the assassination of JFK or the 9/11
tragedy. I was outside on the front lawn watching Gordon
and Kelly fix something on the car. Gretchen came out
of the house and said, "Aunt Vicki is on the phone and
wants to talk to you." I hurried into the house, anxious to
visit with my sister. She said, "Dad just died."

I could hardly believe what I heard. My Dad was
very healthy, how could he be dead? She went into a
few details, and then I went out to tell my family that
Grandpa Altepeter was dead. Even now I feel a bit tearful
thinking about it, although it was over thirty years ago.
Dad was a healthy person in spite of abusing his body; he
smoked those nasty Camels and drank too much alcohol.
He would take the caps off bottles with his teeth, and yet

he never went to the dentist. I only remember him being in the hospital one time, when he had a nosebleed that was hard to stop. Mom said he had the constitution of an ox.

My Dad was a creature of habit. Had his coffee in the morning and walked to work every day on the same downtrodden path through a weedy vacant lot. The only thing I remember him and my mom fighting about was his drinking. They never yelled or screamed at each other. Mom would just give him the silent treatment.

He would stay out late at the tavern, and when he came home, no matter how he tried to hide it, you could tell if he had been drinking because he stuttered. Dad had clear diction until he had a beer or two, and then it took him a lot longer to get a sentence out of his mouth.

I kind of likened my Dad to Abraham Lincoln, because he was honest as the day was long. One time we went to a little grocery store in the town of Lily Lake, and on the way home Mom was checking the receipt, and she said, "Mr. Reed forgot to charge us for the coffee." My Dad turned the car around and said, "That man works hard for his money. We need to go back and pay him."

What a wonderful example that was for us girls. We respected our Mom and Dad and would never talk back to them. Also, my Dad never swore; he would say, "Awe Rats," when something went wrong.

Dad could fix absolutely anything, and he had a knack for inventing things. One time he made a rotating hot dog cooker out of long spikes. We laughed at some of his concoctions, but today I often see something similar at hot dog stands. He should have patented it.

During my early married years, I lived in St. Charles, Illinois. One afternoon, I was caring for our first baby, Gretchen, when there was a knock at our apartment door. Surprise, it was Dad. He was then working at Modern Dairy in Elgin, Illinois, about twenty miles from St. Charles. I invited him in, and he did a little baby talk with Gretchen, used the bathroom, and sat for a few minutes. He clearly wanted to talk about something, but he just didn't have the words, nor did I. After a short time, he got up and said, "I just needed to use the bathroom." So he went twenty miles out of his way to do this? I think not.

Many years later, I returned back to college to become a counselor, and one of the assignments was to explore our own issues before trying to help others. I did what was called "inner-child work"; it was meant to identify and resolve childhood feelings. To do this, I planned a visit to the cemetery to converse with my Dad. I think after all those years we finally had that father/daughter conversation. He may not have had the words to express it, but we girls all knew he loved us.

Mom Decides to Date

Anita

When our parents married, Mom was sixteen years old, and Dad was nearly thirty-six. Mom always told us the story of when she attended grade school, and George, already a workingman, had been in an accident. She remembered her whole class praying for him daily and how strange she thought it was that several years later she would marry this man.

Their marriage lasted for forty-three years until Dad unexpectedly passed away. Now, for the first time ever, Mom was alone. She had always lived with someone—initially, her parents, and then Dad. She remained in the family homestead for a short time before deciding she wanted to put it up for sale. She could no longer tolerate the quiet of the empty house, void of laughter and companionship. My apartment lease was soon up, so the family decided that Mom would move in with me and my first husband, Jackie, and our toddler, Sarah.

The house in Virgil sold quickly, and we signed our lease for a three-bedroom, ground-floor apartment in Batavia. Shortly after we moved into the apartment, Mom announced that she would begin dating.

Soon, she had befriended a man in the apartment down the hall, and they started going uptown to the pub several evenings a week. The man was quite handsome, and Mom saw great potential in him until she learned that he was gay and they were competing against each other for attention from the same men at the bar. They continued to be friends, but Mom decided this time she would try her luck with the *Bonni Buyer* newspaper companionship ads.

She met a nice widow man who was very thoughtful, held the doors, and was very attentive, even bringing flowers on occasion. He seemed perfect until one evening he did not appear for their date because he had a last minute issue with a family member. Mom waited patiently, and he did not show, nor did he call. The next day he called and explained that his daughter had stopped by to visit and he could not leave. Mom was enraged, but since this was the first time it had happened, she quickly forgave him, especially since he stopped by later bearing chocolates along with his apology. They continued to be companions to each other for six months. Several times he would not show up for their date, and finally Mom grew tired of this, and they parted ways.

Mom swiftly returned to the ads. This time she met Mr. B, a chubby gentleman who was always pleasant to be around. He was an on-site handyman at the nearby Mooseheart, a home for families that lost their financial provider. Unable to support themselves, these families lived in dorm-style housing, underwritten by the loyal order of the Moose. Mr. B and Mom would do free activities at the Moose and go on picnics and to inexpensive places because Mr. B was on a fixed income. He also had a huge white cockatiel that chattered endlessly. Mom was unimpressed by the bird's noise and even more unimpressed by the feathers that were always in his kitchen. Needless to say, this relationship did not last long either.

Shortly after the relationship with Mr. B ended, Mom; my husband, Jackie; and I were all home one Friday evening watching a late movie. As usual, I fell asleep on the couch. At about midnight, I awoke to the sound of the apartment door closing. Still groggy from my sleep, I asked Jackie what was going on. He replied that Mom had just left on a date. He proceeded to tell me that Mom had received a call from somebody she had corresponded with via the want ads. They were going out to have a couple of drinks and to get to know each other. Now fully alert, I was livid with him for letting her go out so late and furious with Mom for being so foolish.

I was beside myself with worry as the hours ticked away and she was not home. She had to be to work in the morning by seven o'clock, so she should have been home by now. Finally, at 5:30 in the morning, the door quietly opened, and Mom snuck in carrying her shoes in hopes of not waking me. I bolted from the couch toward her and in a boisterous voice proceeded to quiz her. She had been at the bar having drinks when they decided to go to his house to have some whiskey. I could not believe my ears. She had gone out after midnight with a stranger and then went to his house. After lecturing her and making her promise never to behave this way again, she changed her clothes and went to work, her head pounding all morning.

Finally, after several more dating experiences, Mom met Gilbert, who would eventually become her second husband.

Vicki

I was not as privy to mom's dating escapades as my younger sister, Nita. Of course, mother would say that was not the case. She couldn't get away with anything because of the grapevine between her daughters.

I remember Mr. B, who worked at Mooseheart in North Aurora. Mom found it necessary for us to take a tour of the complex, guided by Mr. B. The whole family, including all of our young children, dutifully trudged behind him as he took us through the cottages, school, and working farm. We did, however, get to see an amazingly beautiful chapel. The tour ended at Mr. B's residence, which was a small kitchenette apartment that he shared with his parakeet. He was also the most creative of mother's dates, as he loved to make signs on huge pieces of paper for birthdays and holidays. Mother insisted we take the signs to work and have them displayed. I did it for Mom's sake, but I was embarrassed because the one that I got to take had the word *Thanksgiving* misspelled. I would do anything for Mom.

I recall one evening receiving a call from Nita because Mom was becoming reckless with her dating. The discussion was about whether we needed to talk to her about the use of condoms. It had been quite some time since Mom was in the dating arena, and we were concerned that she might need to be brought up to date on STDs, etc. This was a new concept for us, since mother never had "the talk" with us about sex, now how could we have this talk with her?

I think Nita started this talk, and Linda and I reinforced the information during our phone calls. This was the first time I could see that the tables were turning, and soon our roles with Mother would be changing from the one being taken care of to the caregiver.

Mother continued her dating, trying to hone her newfound skills. She had never been a drinker, and now we found her drinking the occasional cocktail socially. This dating side to mother was a new one for us to see. She had always been just Mom, who stayed at home and took care of us.

She married a second time to Gilbert, who was a chef and loved organ music, and then had a third marriage with Walter. My mother was not a floozy, but she was a very social person and required companionship. After the deaths of Gil and Walter, she moved into Asbury Towers in North Aurora, and her final home was at Plum Landing in Aurora. There she made many friends, especially a few gentlemen who required daily hugs. My mother was a very loving woman with a heart that would not stop giving until it finally gave out on her.

Linda

Mother was one of those people who never wanted to be alone. She dated several men after Dad passed away. All of them had their own little quirks, but Mom enjoyed their companionship. Mother was a very strong woman. I don't know how she managed to survive the death of three husbands and still move forward.

Mom lived with Anita for a while until I moved to Batavia with my family, and it was decided that Mom would move into our house. I can remember her and my daughter, Trina, giving each other dating advice. I would have loved to be a fly on that wall listening to their conversations.

Later in life when Mom moved to the retirement homes, she would always meet some interesting gentleman and would share his biography with us.

When mother reached her late eighties, she declared she was not looking to get married again. Our whole family gave a sigh of relief!

Ruth

In the months following Dad's death, Mom was very lonely. She told me she was glad she had a job and something to keep her busy during the day. She hated to go home at night to her empty house. She said she cried all the time. After a while, Mom decided to sell our family home, and she went to live with my sister Anita and her family.

Because I lived in Missouri with my family, I did not have much contact with Mom during her dating era. We did, however, have several visits from Mom and her new husband, Gil. Gil was a retired chef who used to work in downtown Chicago. After Mom met him, she decided he needed a makeover. She took him to her personal beauty salon, where he got a new, short hairstyle and a kinky, curly perm, which looked identical to hers! Once, when we were driving our car behind theirs, we noticed that it looked like we were following a car driven by two large gray poodles.

On Gil's first visit, he commented on my lack of pans and proper cooking utensils. On his second visit, he brought all his own paraphernalia from home. He loved cooking and especially enjoyed baking for us. One day Mom and I were visiting, and Gil seemed especially bored, so I asked John to entertain him. John took him out to our messy garage and asked him to help sort out piles of nuts, bolts, screws, and nails to put in specific jars. Finally, Gil looked at John and said, "This isn't very much fun."

The last time we saw Gil, he lay dying in the hospital. When we arrived there, he was nonresponsive and in a coma. John prayed over him, shared the Lord with him, and then said, "Gil, would you like to receive Jesus?"

Gil suddenly rose up and loudly said, "Yes." He then settled down and went back into the coma. John baptized him from with a glass of water that was at his bedside.

Mom married once again after Gil's death to Walter Colsten. I knew Walter least of all. They came down to visit us only once. Walter was always neatly dressed, wearing a suit and tie on Sundays. He had a glass eye and a hip replacement. He was a good conversationalist and very knowledgeable on many subjects. Mom was a good wife to Walter and cared for him until his death.

After outliving three husbands, we kidded Mom about number four. She would always say that she would only be interested in a younger man. She didn't want to have to take care of any more senior citizens!

Helen

No kid thinks their mother should be dating! After Dad died, it must have been a very difficult time for Mom—it was the first time she was ever alone. I was busy raising my children in Geneseo, quite a distance away from Virgil, so I had no idea what she was going through or what my sisters were going through. Years later, she told me how lonesome she had been. She went to work in a T-shirt factory in St. Charles. This was the first job she ever had outside the home, except for cleaning the priest's house.

Change is difficult at any age, and several changes at one time are extremely unsettling. Mom sold the house in Virgil, where she had lived for forty some years, and moved to Batavia, Illinois. She had lived in Virgil ever since her birth—that's where her friends and relatives lived, and that's where she knew all her neighbors and their families. She moved in with my sister Anita and her family.

Fluffy, Funny, and
Fabulous

It was then that Mother decided to shop for a husband. Mom came from an era where a woman needed to be married. It seemed to us girls that she should have been happy with the company of her children and grandchildren, so it was difficult for us to see her in this new role.

I wasn't there for her day-to-day adventures, but occasionally she would tell me of a new person she met. She would bring her current beau with her on her visits to Geneseo. Each had his little foibles. One sported yard sale rings on every finger; another was what she termed "a hippy" because he had long hair. They were short and fat or tall and skinny. It was hard to tell what kind of guy she would bring to visit. One time my son asked, "Grandma, why don't you find someone like Grandpa?"

She quickly replied, "When you get to be my age, the pickings get slim."

Back Together Because of Mom

Anita

Mom was almost eighty-five years old but still in great health for her age. And mentally, she was as sharp as ever. Sure, she had a few problems with her breathing and swelling of her legs, but that was because she wasn't getting enough exercise. She just needed to get out of her house a little more. Vicki, Linda, Helen, and I decided to take her walking at the outlet mall. Mom was passionate about shopping. She always wore perfectly matched outfits and accessories and could wear any bright color imaginable because of her perfect white hair. Taking her shopping would definitely be good for her. She made it to several stores until finally she was exhausted and her breathing was labored. She had to go home and put her feet up and rest.

On Monday, Mom decided she should go to the doctor. This was not unusual for Mom because she enjoyed the social visits that she seemed to have with her doctor. They always joked, and Mom would tell him that a hug from him was all she ever needed to cure whatever was troubling her that trip. This day was different. He immediately sent her to the hospital for some tests because her heart didn't sound quite right. Linda had the afternoon available, so she was the one who accompanied Mom. At about 4:00 p.m. I got a frantic, panic-stricken call. "Mom is going to need quadruple bypass surgery," Linda explained, barely able to bring herself to say the words.

I summoned Vicki, and we rushed to the hospital to meet Linda. I was so afraid, but also I was feeling such guilt. Why hadn't I taken off work to go with Mom? After all, it was my responsibility to make sure Mom was okay, and I made Linda do my job.

Mom always told me Linda was the fragile one and needed to be protected, and now she was alone listening to these doctors tell her our mother needed to be transferred to Sherman Hospital immediately because she was in danger of heart failure and could die.

Vicki and I arrived at the hospital at the same time, unsure what lay in store for our family. Linda was amazingly composed and in control of everything. I was so proud of her and realized at that moment that she possessed an inner strength that I had not seen before. She had taken very detailed notes when speaking to the doctors and included some diagrams to help explain to us what was going on. Once the three of us talked the situation over, dried our tears, and composed ourselves, we knew what had to be done. We banded together and went to face our dear Mom.

Dreading even saying the words *heart surgery*, we gingerly reached her bedside. We were all amazed and shocked as she told us, without hesitation, that she was going to have the surgery. She explained to us how bad she had been feeling and did not want to continue this way. She was willing to take any risk as long as she was not a burden to her family. She asked us individually what we felt, and as a team we all agreed that the surgery was best.

Her surgery happened three days later. The night before, everyone came to her room in the IC unit at Sherman Hospital. All of her beloved grandchildren stopped by to wish her luck and express their love to her. There were hugs, tears, and laughter, and Mom made sure to spend a few private moments with each individual who came into the room and remind them how much she loved them and how much she appreciated them coming to see her. Mom was the glue that held us all together, so it was very important and comforting to each of us as she also assured everyone that she was not through fighting yet and the surgery was going to be fine.

After they all left, the sisters and their husbands remained and talked and prayed. Mom wanted to be reassured that she was making the right decision and that she was not going to die. In our hearts and minds, we all knew the high risk this surgery would be for an eighty-five-year-old woman, but we also knew that this was our Mom, and God would protect her.

The morning of the surgery, all five of the sisters and several of the brothers-in-law arrived at the hospital early to be with Mom as she was prepped for her ordeal. The head nurse assigned to the operation stopped by to explain the procedure should take three to four hours. Every hour we could call a special phone number, and there would be a recording from her on the progress. When the nurse left, John prayed over all of us, and after all of our *love yous*, Mom was whisked away, and we were sentenced to waiting the hours for her surgery to be over so we could be reunited with her.

I loved all my sisters and their spouses, but I was never comfortable being around them as a large group. Whenever we had family gatherings of everyone, I would try to spend as little time as possible. I always felt like, being the youngest, they looked down on me. They were all successful, smart, fit in with each other, and enjoyed each other's company. How could I compete? After all, I was younger, fat, not pretty like all of them, never wore makeup, lived in Aurora, and had very little in common with them as a group. I was close to Vicki and Linda, but not when we were all together. I felt like the black sheep of the family.

As much as I dreaded Mom's surgery, I dreaded spending that day with my family. I armed myself with schoolbooks, a CD, and earphones so I could exclude myself from their company as much as possible. I did not want to be there with them, feeling like a stranger in my own family, but I could not bear to leave the room either because it was my connection with Mom's condition.

Every hour I would dutifully dial the number we had been given and report to the group what was going on. Hour one—things were going well. Hour two—things were still on target. Hour three—all is still well. *Maybe this will be over soon and Mom will be in recovery.* Hour four—complications reported. They found more blockage than expected, and the doctor would have to do more repair. *This is dangerous because she should not be under the anesthesia this long. What if they can't do the repairs? We can't lose our precious mom. She is the glue that holds us all together. God, please give us strength and give the doctor a steady hand and be with our Mom.* Hour Five—no update. Fear, panic, tears, and prayers set in. *Lord God, we need our Mom. We can't survive without her. Please Lord. We beg of you, give us strength. Please Lord, heal our Mom.* Hour six—I gathered all my inner strength and pressed the buttons on the phone, holding my breath, afraid of what words might come from the other side. *Hallelujah! Thank you, God!* They had successfully completed the repairs and were getting ready to close. Mom would be in recovery within the hour, and the doctor would be down to speak to the family then.

The clock ticked away the seconds as if they were hours. Nobody talked or dared leave to even go to the bathroom as we waited for that all-important briefing from the doctor. Finally, the short, visibly exhausted man appeared in the waiting room. Surgery had been rough. Mom was under the anesthesia longer than they had hoped, and now it was a wait-and-see situation.

"The next twenty-four hours will be crucial," the doctor explained.

She had suffered so much trauma that, due to her age, the medical staff found it necessary to induce a coma so her body could heal. She was on breathing apparatus and bound in an all-body suit that would pulse on and off to keep the circulation going so she did not get bedsores. We could go in and see her but were warned not to be shocked and to remember that she could hear us so we were not to agitate her by trying to talk to her.

When I was young, my dream was to become a nurse. I was always fascinated by the machine that the human body was, but I also had compassion and empathy for the people who occupied those bodies. I started my college career by taking medical assistant classes but quit after three semesters. Later I, again, attempted to fulfill my dream by taking nursing classes in the evening. But life got in the way, and I could not quit my job to do the necessary internship, which was only offered during the day. Along the way I took classes and became a certified nursing assistant and worked weekends and evenings for a hospice. I had a client who had advanced stages of multiple sclerosis and several others who were at home waiting for the Lord to take them home and relieve their suffering from the cancer in their bodies. I had also done some work in a nursing home and in a hospital, so I thought I had seen most things. I was very wrong.

The family walked down the short hall in the ICU to the corner room where we had talked and joked with Mom hours earlier. Before we even approached the room, we could hear the rhythmic in and out of the respirator that was doing the breathing for Mom. Glancing over, I saw the tears form in Linda's eyes and the panicked expression on her face. John had his arm around Ruth, fearing that she would faint, and Helen, usually talkative and upbeat, was eerily silent. Vicki and I, wearing our face of bravado, led the way.

Just as the doctor had described, Mom was shrouded in a mummy-like full body suit. Her eyes were still taped shut from the surgery, and her face was a strange shade of blue and purple. We all stood motionless, taking in the grotesque figure before us that was once our beautiful, vibrant mother. John went to the foot of the bed and gathered us together to whisper some prayers for all of us and for Mom's speedy recovery. One by one, everyone left the room. I stood frozen, not knowing what to do. I wanted to hug Mom, even shake her and scream at her how much I needed her and that she couldn't give up the fight. I wanted to curl up in a ball and cry uncontrollably till she somehow would comfort me and let me know it would be okay. But I could do none of this, so I sent my thoughts to a better time and place.

It was Christmas many years earlier. We were doing a family gift exchange at Linda's house and were playing a game to determine who could open their presents first. Divided teams had to take rolls of toilet paper and wrap Mom and our stepfather, Walter, into mummies. The first team to finish wrapping their mummy from head to toe would be declared the winner.

With Christmas carols coming from the CD player in the background, the competition began. Laughter, cheers, and lighthearted taunting of the other team ensued.

When the mummies were complete, it was clear that Mummy Mom was the winner. The team had managed to cover every inch of her with the toilet paper bandages. After it was over, with a couple of quick gestures, Mom broke free of the binding and emerged, beautifully clothed in her new, bright-red Christmas sweater and matching accessories that she had arrived at the house in. More cheers and hugs for the team and the mummy, and on to celebrate the birth of Christ.

The memory was so real at that moment that it caused me to glance over at Mom's lifeless body, hoping that this hospital ordeal would become a memory as Mom shed the bandages and emerged as the triumphant victor, just like in our game years earlier. Of course, this was not the case, and I was jolted back to reality by the rhythms of the respirator, in and out.

Finally, I left the room to rejoin the family in the waiting room. Everyone was in shock; we were not able to verbalize to one another what we had just witnessed. Exhausted, we made plans to go home and get some rest. We had a schedule set up to call the hospital every four hours to check on Mom. If anything changed, we would notify the rest of the family.

Mom made it through the first critical phase, the night. Plans were made to go back to the hospital later that morning. We all arrived at various times during the morning, briefly going in and out of Mom's room, staring at the cocoon that contained our mom, waiting for her to emerge or for the doctor to tell us they would be freeing her from her prison.

Finally, after three days of this, we received the news we wanted. They were going to remove her from the respirator and see if she could breathe on her own. Success; next, they would remove the feeding tube—another success.

On Sunday, Ruth and John informed us that they would have to go back to Missouri to tend to their business. Helen also needed to return to her counseling job. Mom appeared to be stable, and we all knew there was a long road ahead before she would return to her home in North Aurora.

Linda had been down in the gift store passing away the time between visits to Mom's bedside when she saw a tapestry on the wall. It was a picture of a family that had been woven into a wall hanging. She gathered the information to share with the other sisters.

"Wouldn't it be wonderful to have a tapestry made for Mom?" she shared.

Mother was always proud and almost arrogant as she told all of her friends, and anyone else who would listen, the tales of her five daughters. In her eyes, we were perfect.

On Sunday afternoon we met at Linda's to have that perfect picture taken. It took five or six tries to get us all looking forward, with the right smile and our eyes open, but finally the persistence of the cameraman paid off. We agreed on a picture that was a good representation of all five of us. At that moment we did not know that the tapestry would become Mom's most prized possession in her life and that she would even be blanketed in it when she went to her grave.

Looking at the final picture that day, I realized that I did belong in this family. I truly was the fifth piece of the chain. I did have something to offer, and this ordeal with Mother had somehow cemented the relationship of the sisters forever.

Vicki

Ours had always been a close-knit family, even though the range in age from the eldest to the youngest was pretty significant. Mom had brought us up that way. I had heard stories from other families of feuding family members who would not talk to one another for years. I always thought how terrible that would be as Mom instilled in all of us the importance of family. That being said, I could not foresee the future I would have with my siblings and how we would work together as a unit in the final years of mother's life and the years thereafter.

Mother, at the age of eighty-five, would be undergoing triple bypass surgery. Where had the years gone? I had never really noticed that she was aging and her body was starting to fail her. There was much communication over the phone lines, and I was happy that all my sisters would be at the hospital for Mother's surgery.

It was finally the day for Mom's heart surgery. She was in great spirits, as was always the case in any endeavor Mom undertook. Mom was always an optimistic, confident person, and she always exuded an aura of control about her. She made us believe that everything was going to be okay, and she could not have continued to live in her current condition. Her life could be brought back to her previous level of living.

Then we waited, trying to consume our time with light conversation, reading, snacking, and doing crossword puzzles—a skill learned from Mother. The time passed slowly, hour upon hour. We reluctantly went down to the cafeteria in shifts, maintaining our vigil and our strength for the continuation of the waiting period. The final update came, and we found out that Mom had come through the surgery after additional blockage was found and repaired. The life-threatening pressure was off. We awaited our visit with the surgeon and directions for her care going forward.

Finally, after what seemed like days, we were told we could go into see Mom. She would not be awake, as she was put into a coma to speed the healing process. Even when she finally was awake, she would have a breathing tube in and would not be able to talk. We should be very careful not to agitate her because not being able to talk or express herself would be agitation enough.

As I approached her bedside, I saw a cocoon-encased woman lying in the bed. She was sleeping on an inflatable mattress atop the hospital bed. Her appearance was yellow in color, and her whole body looked swollen. I was really shocked. I felt the need to be with her as difficult as it was to see her in this unresponsive state, but this was my mother. Wasn't she always there for me? I would try to remain strong; my family needed that from me.

The following days were filled with staggered visits to the hospital and seeing family intermittently throughout as Mother's healing process slowly progressed.

> "For I know the plans I have for you," declares the Lord, "plans to prosper you and not to harm you, plans to give you hope and a future."
>
> Jeremiah 29:11 (NIV)

What more can I say? God's plan unfolds daily. From here forward, things would change, starting with Mom's long rehabilitation causing her to become more dependent on her children. This dependence on us was most difficult for her because no one was as strong and independent as my mother. It was her job to care for others. The reverse would be difficult for her.

Our family started to work like a well-oiled machine, communicating on Mother's care daily. I called Mom every morning, Ruth called every evening, and Helen on Saturday, plus the many additional calls and visits Mom received from Nita and Linda. Nita took the key role as mother's right hand, and her common sense and nursing skills became a blessing to the family. She became communication central for the family, and to this day I do not know how we could have kept it all together without her. Mom knew and appreciated this too.

Linda

Mother's surgery was so difficult for the sisters to deal with. She had always been so healthy!

We would get together with Mom and have such wonderful times laughing, teasing, and reminiscing. Mom was always the life of the party and such a good sport. Seeing her after her surgery lying in the hospital bed practically lifeless was more than we could handle. Anita, always the strong one, took on that role once again. She was the liaison between the doctors and nurses concerning Mother's health and rehab.

Mom was still in rehab when Christmas arrived. Christmas was one of Mother's favorite holidays, and we were going to be sure the family surrounded her to help her celebrate. I decorated a bright-red hat for her to wear, and she wore one of her Christmas sweaters. For a woman who just had major heart surgery, she looked radiant. Her beloved daughters and grandchildren were once again at her side, not only celebrating the birth of Christ, but also rejoicing that God had gifted us with our mother's survival.

Ruth

Once again, my husband and I were making an emergency trip to Illinois. I received a phone call from my sister Anita, who informed me that Mom needed open-heart surgery as soon as possible.

I was in a panic because of the seriousness of Mom's situation. She was eighty-five years old at this time. Thank

God my husband remained calm and comforting during the long trip while I cried uncontrollably and had a big meltdown. I felt tremendous guilt because of how I had neglected Mom over the years. After my family moved to Missouri, it felt like we were a million miles away, almost like we were in another country. I got wrapped up in all of the things involved with raising my children, running a business, and the demands of life. Although I dearly loved and felt close to my Mother and sisters, I had little communication with them. It was not unusual for me to forget Mom's birthday or, I am ashamed to say, even Mother's Day. But now I was being drawn back to Illinois and back to my family.

I know God brings seasons in our lives. There is a time to laugh and a time to cry, a time to rejoice and a time to mourn, a time to be born and a time to die. Mom was in the fall season of her life. Unbeknownst to her, she was once again drawing her daughters back to her and back to each other.

As we sped toward our destination, I looked out the car window and observed the splendor of the brightly colored fall leaves and the gleaming golden beauty of the tall cornstalks swaying in the gentle breeze. I could only imagine the smile on the proud farmer's face as he gazed across the fields at the bounty of his harvest. I was reminded of past falls when we all gathered for our Mother's annual Thanksgiving meal. I could remember the wonderful aroma of the golden-brown turkey sitting on our dinner table, surrounded by heaps of mashed potatoes, yams, cornbread, and many other delicious dishes prepared by our Mother for us to enjoy. Mom was the heart of our home and the cement that held our family together. Though the seasons of life quickly pass, we forever carry the fond memories of those times and of the people we love.

When we arrived in Illinois, it was great to see my sisters again. We have always been a source of strength and encouragement to each other. In the morning, all of the sisters and husbands made the pilgrimage to the hospital to visit with Mom until her time for surgery. We all tried to be upbeat and lighthearted for her sake, but inside each one of us was brokenhearted. I kissed my Mom right before she was wheeled into surgery, and I patted her fluffy, curly, pure-white hair as I loved to do. I realized I was not ready to lose my Mom. If God would give me another chance, I would become the kind of daughter my wonderful Mother deserved.

Mom's surgery seemed to take forever. We all waited in the recovery room, along with several ladies who were Mom's friends from church. My sister Vicki brought homemade Rice Krispie squares. They were, of course, a comfort for all of us. After a while, we took a break downstairs to the cafeteria, where we had coffee, soda, and snacks. During this tense time, I think we all felt a renewed sense of kinship. We really did rekindle that bond of love for each other that we had experienced in our childhood during a much different season of Mom's life.

At one point during our long vigil, my husband, John, went off by himself to pray for Mom. He asked the Lord to not only preserve her but to allow her to live at least another five more years with her daughters. God gave him a vision of Mom, recovered and sitting in a chair! He privately told this to me, and it gave me much comfort because so many times in the past God had faithfully revealed our future to us.

Although this was an extremely difficult season for all of us girls and our Mother, it was also, in retrospect, a wonderful time. Our sweet Mother did recover and went on to have many more adventures and much happiness in her life.

I never again took her for granted but began the routine of faithfully calling her almost every evening after nine o'clock. We became extremely close, both as mother and daughter and also as good friends. We talked about everything you could imagine, from utter silliness to very personal matters. I am so grateful to God for giving me this marvelous second chance with my mom and also with my sisters. We have been reunited as sisters again and have rallied around Mom and around each other.

Helen

The sisters had always gathered together for happy events—birthdays, weddings, and shopping trips—but the most bonding time was during Mom's heart surgery. Mom had always been fairly healthy, and only a couple of weeks before the surgery, she had been on a shopping spree with several of us girls. So, consequently, it was quite a shock to find out she had heart problems. Even today, as I look back, it seems somewhat surreal. That was the first time I ever thought about one day not having a Mom. It was also a time that I realized that my sisters would always be there for me and for each other.

I got a call informing me that Mom was going to have heart surgery. I informed my workplace that I had to be gone for a couple of days, and off I went to be with my sisters and my Mom.

The day of the surgery, we were at the hospital early so we could visit with Mom. I remember we were all walking alongside her as they wheeled her down the corridor to the operating room. One by one we hugged and kissed her and told her we loved her. Then we waited and watched the clock, assuring each other that she would be okay, but deep down we were dreading the worst. We were in the waiting area and every hour would get an update on how our Mother's surgery was progressing. We were afraid to leave for fear we would miss an important update. We finally took a break for lunch and made a stroll through the hospital gift shop. Ruth spotted a tapestry that could be customized with a personal photo. She mentioned that this might be a nice gift for Mom if we could take a photo of all us girls. We all halfheartedly agreed but were preoccupied with fear and apprehension at the time.

Little did we know, days later, when we were posing for the photo, that our Mother would treasure that tapestry for the rest of her life. Mother recovered from that surgery, but it took its toll on her. As I look back, it was probably the beginning of her health problems. She moved to a couple different apartments after that, and she always displayed that tapestry in a prominent place so she could introduce all her visitors to "her girls."

Years later, just before they closed her casket, "her girls" tucked the tapestry around her body to be buried with her.

Asbury Towers and Plum Landing

Anita

*M*om recovered from her heart surgery and, after many grueling months of physical therapy, was able to return to her home in North Aurora. She was as sharp as ever mentally, but the trauma to her body had taken its toll.

She was using a walker when she came home, and the doctor told her to continue until she got stronger. He also told her to get exercise, which was never one of Mom's favorite pastimes. She had worked hard raising her family and doing all the required chores that needed to be done, but she was never one of those people who would go for health walks or do calisthenics.

Stubborn and unwilling to obey the doctor's advice, Mom used the excuse that she now used a walker and was therefore a cripple and should be exempt from exercise. She would get up in the morning and gingerly make her way to the bathroom and then to her favorite chair in the living room, where she would remain until she needed to go to the bathroom. Lunch was furnished by Meals on Wheels, so she rarely even had to go to the kitchen.

This pattern went on for months, although all the sisters tried to get her to be more active. Linda found a woman's group for her to join, even securing a ride for her, but Mom decided she didn't like the group. Daughters, sons-in-law, and grandchildren would stop by and tempt her to leave the house by offering to take her to supper or to Fashion Bug to go shopping. Even these activities did not coax her into becoming active. Finally, we had a family meeting of the sisters. We determined that it was time to convince Mom to sell her house and move to an independent senior-living apartment complex. She could be around other people who were her own age and had similar life experiences. There would be activities and also someone in the building if she needed some assistance.

Vicki, Linda, and I were the ones designated to approach the subject with her. One evening we appeared at her door with carry-out soup and sandwiches. After eating, I started the conversation. Mom's first thoughts were not positive. She had no plans of ever moving again, and once, years earlier, she had gone to a free lunch at one of those places, and it was very expensive. She was not going to throw away her life savings. No, she was happy right here in her own chair. We explained that we would look at several places and find the right one for her and at the right price. She agreed, grudgingly, to think about it. When we left her house, we immediately called Ruth and Helen and filled them in. Ruth was to call Mom later that night for an evening chat and steer the conversation so she could reaffirm our earlier talking points. Helen was to call on Saturday morning, which was her usual time, and also voice her agreement.

After a week, Mom announced that she was willing to consider moving as long as we found a place that would not cost an arm and a leg. Vicki and I already started the search in anticipation of this decision. We selected two complexes—one in St. Charles, and the second, called Asbury Towers, was in North Aurora. The Towers were conveniently located close to my home and work and also close to Linda's home.

With Mother in tow, Linda, Vicki, and I went to tour Asbury. We were greeted by a wonderfully friendly woman. She explained all that the Towers had to offer and showed us an apartment. The two-bedroom, unfurnished unit would be perfect for Mom because it would allow room for all of her clothes and she could take along enough of her favorite furniture to make it feel like her home. She would have room for a small refrigerator and some snack foods, bur her three meals would be eaten in the dining hall with all the other residents. Throughout the day, activities, such as bingo, cards, and crafts, would be offered. In addition, there were many areas in which to sit and visit. A large TV room, a library, and a small exercise room were also on site. Mail was delivered to the first floor and put in the mail slots by 10:00 a.m. so the residents could walk down and pick up their mail and chat before lunch. Linda, Vicki, and I were all three ready to move in. We thought it would be perfect. A few days later, Mom asked us to put her house on the market. It sold quickly, and she was off to her new life.

It was a struggle for Mom to get used to this place. Asbury Towers was a remodeled Holiday Inn, and she needed to take the elevator to her third-floor apartment. We discovered that Mom had never really been on an elevator alone, and she found the buttons confusing. To make things more difficult, there were two different elevators on either end of the third floor. Both elevators came out in different areas, so it would confuse Mom if she took the wrong one and arrived at a spot different than she had anticipated. We put a wreath on her door so she could find her apartment, put a sign in the elevator stating what floor various things were on, and made sure when we were with her to always take the same route. As time went on, she adjusted and made many friends. Soon, she was one of the most popular women because she also had a kind word for everyone and was always willing to help anyone new. She also became the envy of the other women because she always dressed so nicely and had matching accessories, courtesy of Ruth and John's jewelry business.

Eventually, she caught the eye of one of the few male residents, Orin. He was a quiet, well-mannered gentleman who opened doors and would oftentimes stop by to watch movies at Mom's apartment. He was losing his hearing, so the couple would usually sit in silence until one or both of them would fall asleep on the couch. Orin would then toddle back to his own apartment and call Mom so they could talk on the phone before bedtime. The phone acted like an amplifier, so their phone conversations were much longer and more detailed than their face-to-face encounters. This relationship lasted for quite some time until Orin became ill and had to move closer to his family for care.

Mom kept in touch with his family, even attending his birthday party at his son's home. I drove Mom to the party in Downers Grove. When we arrived, Orin was seated in a wheelchair wearing a new pale-blue sweater that earlier that day had been given to him as a birthday present. Mother's comment on how dapper he looked in that shade of blue brought a huge Cheshire cat grin to his tired and shallow face. It was obvious that Orin was approaching his death, although the words were never shared aloud. This would be the last celebration this group would have together, so they treated it as a solemn but still-festive celebration of Orin's life. Mother and I both felt honored to be part of the evening. We attended his funeral one week later.

Shortly after this loss, Mom had to endure another major event. After Christmas, each of the residents of Asbury Towers received a letter stating that the complex would be closing in two months. The residents and their families would be scheduled to meet individually with the management, who would offer them other solutions to help accommodate their living arrangements. Mother and all the other residents were heartbroken and enraged at the same time. They had formed deep ties with each other and had no desire to abruptly be forced from their homes.

We contacted the two local newspapers with this story of Asbury Tower closing and the resident's plight.

Mom became an instant celebrity. She was interviewed by both papers, appearing the next morning on the front page, complete with a picture of herself sitting in her apartment with three of her daughters: Linda, Vicki, and I. The story was picked up by the ten o'clock evening news. They arrived the next evening for a live broadcast from the Towers. Mom appeared before the camera with all the poise and beauty that had become her trademark. Her brightly colored blouse with matching turquoise earrings and necklace accentuated her snow-white hair and played perfectly to the camera's eye. She was radiant as she explained in a clear, firm voice that it was not right to push these old people into the street with no warning and few options. Although the publicity caused quite a stir in the area and was quite the gossip item for many days at the lunch tables, Asbury still shut its doors, and Mom had to find a new residence.

After doing another search, we selected Plum Landing—a retirement community that had been designed with seniors as the focus. The apartments were large, with a small balcony that overlooked the Fox River. The selling point for Mom was the built-in closets that had more space than even she needed for her huge wardrobe.

Several of the other residents from Asbury would also be moving to the same place, so Mom would not lose all of her friends. Mother grew to think of Plum Landing as home and became one of the favorite residents. She was loved by the staff and residents alike.

Vicki

After Mom's surgery, she made it very apparent that she wanted to go home; however, there would have to be another step in between because she was not fully recovered and able to care for herself. Nita, Linda, and I had to look for an interim facility to provide this care until she regained her strength. We chose Rosewood in St. Charles.

It was a nice, clean, and beautifully decorated intermediate care and nursing home. Mother hated the thought of it, but the doctor and her daughters assured her that it would, hopefully, be a short stay. Even with the frequent visits from her family and the knowledge of this being short-term, she really hated it. The day she was finally well enough to leave, her faced beamed with joy and excitement. She was going home.

Preparations had been made by her family to ensure her safety once she had arrived back home in North Aurora. Safety bars and a shower seat had been installed in her bathroom, and we bought her long-handled sponges, aids to help with socks and shoes, and everything her therapist requested to provide her assistance with daily living. She would use a walker to stabilize herself, as she had one foot that was not working as well as it did previously. After we got her a tray that attached to the walker, she was much happier. She could put her food, remote control, phone, crossword book, or whatever she wanted upon it, and it would be handy. Occasionally, I would decorate it with seasonal silk flowers.

After mom's surgery, she was diagnosed with diabetes. She was very defensive about this, but we were told that it was not uncommon for this to happen after a major surgery like Mother had. Using the diabetes blood strip meter was not something Mother was going to do on her own, so that was something her daughters had to learn. I remember the first time I had to prick her finger for the test. She said it didn't hurt; I didn't so much feel good about it, but I knew it was necessary.

We took turns spending nights at Mom's house to make sure she could get out of bed okay, moving to and from the bathroom and throughout her home. She mumbled and cried out during the night, making our evenings less than restful. When we told her about it in the morning, she had no recollection of any dreams or occurrences during the night.

Mother continued to get better, but we could not get her to be active—something her doctor and nurses would try to push her to do. It was as if she lost the desire to really live her life. She became complacent and happy with visits from her family only. Past friendships were no longer important to her. She was no longer the "social butterfly" of the family. The family thought it was best that she move from her home to a senior facility where she could be around other people her own age and be in an environment where there were activities for seniors. We wanted her to start living her life again and regaining her independence. We weren't sure if we would meet resistance from Mother or not. It would have to be very clear that this was not a nursing home!

After researching and visiting the numerous senior centers, we all settled on Asbury Towers in North Aurora. It was a renovated motel, so Mother would actually have two adjoining rooms that would be set up as living quarters and sleeping quarters with a small kitchenette containing a microwave and small refrigerator. Her meals would be provided in the elegant dining room.

This was the start of Mother never cooking for herself again, which was the envy of all of us girls. We bought bright rose-colored paint for her living home and a beautiful, floral sleeper sofa for guests to sleep on for those overnight stays. The tapestry of her daughters was proudly displayed on the wall; Asbury Towers was now home. Now we just had to help her gain her confidence in finding her way around and utilizing the elevator. That may sound minor, but this was a whole new environment for Mom. It didn't take her long to adjust and make many new friends. She was proud of her new place, and they chose to show her unit to people who were looking to move into Asbury Towers. It became a showplace, like the showroom of a Cadillac dealer. She was quite the lady. There wasn't any challenge my mother would not undertake; however, it might require a little pushing from her girls.

After Asbury Towers announced their closing, or as Mother would say, "They just kicked her to the curb," we settled her into Plum Landing. It was a beautiful facility with a layout accommodating to seniors. The only confusing thing about Plum Landing was that it was built into a hill, so you actually entered on the sixth floor.

Mom's apartment was on the third floor—the one where they showed movies, played Wii, and had numerous parties in the comfortable sitting area. Mom loved to invite her family to meals in the beautiful dining room with the white linen tablecloths, china table service, and complete menu that you could order from, plus scrumptious desserts. Even if Mom was too full to eat her dessert, she took it to-go for later or to share with the first person to visit her. I think Nita got most of the desserts.

Mom was very happy at Plum Landing and made many friends. We loved Plum Landing too. We were especially comforted by the presence of an intercom system. The receptionist, who was really more of a friend, would greet each resident over the intercom every morning and evening, insuring each resident was well. We liked Plum Landing so well that Nita and I always kidded with Mom that when we were old enough we were going to move in too so we could play Bingo, Wii, and dine in elegance. Who knows?

Linda

Mother was experiencing loneliness and probably mild depression when she returned home from her rehab. Despite the fact that she had numerous caregivers checking on her and all of her daughters and family members visiting, we could tell she was still quite lonely. We even suggested she get a dog, which she adamantly refused. We sisters had a meeting and, along with Mother, it was decided that she would be happier at

Asbury Towers, where there would be people around
24/7 for her to mingle with.

We had a huge garage sale, packed her most precious
belongings, and were off to Asbury Towers. Among
her prized possessions was the tapestry of her beloved
daughters and the china cabinet that belonged to Aunt
Mary. Mother entrusted my husband, Jim, to transport
her china cabinet. Little did Jim know that several
months later he would be carefully transporting that
china cabinet to Plum Landing.

Mother's adjustment to Plum Landing was fantastic.
She made many new friends, and she finally found a
place that she could call home. Mother always had some
exciting tale to tell about the Plum Landing happenings.
Plum Landing was an excellent place for mother; we
sisters said that later in life we wouldn't mind being Plum
Landing residents.

Ruth

Mom lived in both Asbury Towers and Plum Landing
after selling her house. We visited most often when she
lived at Plum Landing, which was a beautiful facility.
It was not at all like a traditional nursing home with
robed oldsters sitting in their wheelchairs, staring into
space or sleeping in the halls. Plum Landing Assisted
Living Apartments was an extraordinary and safe place
for seniors who could care for themselves and maintain
a small apartment. There was great camaraderie among
residents who shared similar life experiences and interests
in the fall and winter of their lives.

Meals were served downstairs in an upscale dining room. Mom and her friends would be comfortably seated on upholstered couches and chairs in the foyer while they waited for the double doors of the eatery to swing open. They were then seated at tables covered with cloth tablecloths sporting fabric napkins. After getting their glasses filled with ice cold water and snacking on cheese and crackers provided at each table, the waitresses would bring out menus and take their orders. This was quite a production, and it produced a lovely meal and a delightful time for all. Mom loved to invite her daughters and other family members to dine with her. It was her time to shine as she proudly introduced each one of us to her friends. She was so pleased to have us there and enjoyed showing us off.

Mom had great times at Plum Landing. I phoned Mom every night at nine o'clock. Those calls were laced with tales of her daily adventures—how many quarters she won at bingo, who showed up at exercise class, if the afternoon movie was any good, or who slept through the entire thing. Mostly, she liked to tell me what was going on with her friends and fellow neighbors. Her best friend was Doris, who she felt very close to. She overlooked the fact that Doris seldom made it to exercise class even though she did need to lose weight.

"Maybe she should not take so many naps and walk around more," Mom lamented.

Mom forgave the fact that perhaps Doris drank a smidgen more than she ought. Her two shedding cats kept Doris's clothes covered in hair. This was the reason Mom never went into her apartment but always invited

Doris to her place instead. Doris was a gracious lady, and Mom enjoyed her company.

Bud was the resident ladies' man. Maybe this was because there weren't many men at Plum Landing or maybe, as Mom thought, because he was the only man who owned a car and was still able to drive it. He escorted some of the ladies to the grocery store or chauffeured them to various appointments. Mom assured me that she would never be caught alone with him, even in the elevator, because she didn't trust him. Another annoying issue Mom had with Bud was his habit of going around in the dining room and asking for uneaten desserts. He said he liked to feed them to the ducks, but Mom was pretty sure he ate them himself.

Mom met Orin, and from that point on, she only had eyes for him. When Mom talked about him, she was like a giddy teen girl talking about her crush. I would kid her about him, and she would get all embarrassed and silly acting. It was so cute! Orin seemed to like her as much as she liked him. They spent lots of time together and enjoyed one another's company very much. Mom did have one little issue with Orin and that was the fact that she couldn't remember his name and often called him Owen by mistake. When Orin passed away, it was extremely hard on Mom. In a year's time, she lost her sister Loretta, Doris moved, and Orin died. Mom went through a time of depression, but my sisters—Linda, Vicki, and Anita—were on top of it quickly. They snapped to action and found all sorts of things to get her moving and busy again.

All of my sisters are amazing women. In addition to working full-time jobs and caring for their families, they always had time and energy to care for Mom. Mom was right to be so proud of them! She always said, "What would I do without my girls?"

Helen

Moving from a three-bedroom house to a studio apartment—can you imagine what that would be like? Think of disposing of the majority of your life-long accumulations. Where do you begin? I suppose you would have a lot of sleepless nights sorting it out in your mind. Our mother was very sharp-minded; she asked for advice from her daughters but ultimately made her own decisions. After she developed health problems that slowed her down, she knew it was time to make some hard decisions about moving and getting rid of possessions. She doled out some of her items to family members, sold some at a yard sale, and donated others to Goodwill.

Her house sold quickly, and off she went to Asbury Towers, resigned to make the best of it, albeit a step down in her independence. Mom was a very social person, so it didn't take her long to make acquaintances. She kept in touch with her old friends through letters and cards, although it was noticeable that the visits and correspondence were dwindling down. This is something that happens when you change lifestyles.

As the days and months went by, I'm proud to say that Mom made the transition and was feeling comfortable with her new surroundings and new friends. In fact, she felt so "at home" that when management announced they were closing the doors and residents would need to relocate to other housing, it was quite a shock to Mom. Asbury Towers had become home to her and to the other residents. But all things have a purpose and present an opportunity. It was through a series of events—TV and newspaper interviews—that Mother became the voice of the residents in expressing their shock and disappointment after the closing announcement. She reveled in the limelight. She said, "I never thought in all my years that I would become a spokesperson."

Mother and several of the other residents moved into Plum Landing—a retirement home just a couple of miles down the street from Asbury Towers. This place was more suitable for our mother—it was a little more upscale. This appeared to be a welcomed transition for her. Mother was somewhat of a known entity since her picture had appeared in a couple of newspapers and she had been on the evening news regarding the closing of Asbury Towers. She became part of a group that regularly met in a sitting room by the lobby. We teasingly called it her "Gossip Group," but she corrected us by saying, "We just talk about meaningful things." Mom enjoyed dressing and sporting her jewelry when she had her evening meal in the elegant dining room at Plum Landing.

Mother loved to shop for clothes, and every one of us girls enjoyed taking her to the Dress Barn or the Fashion Bug—her two favorite stores. Ruth always kept her supplied with fancy jewelry and sparkly watches from her jewelry store. Mother had beautiful white hair, so she could wear bright colors and look gorgeous.

Plum Landing was the last stop for our mother. Her health was gradually declining until she needed to have hospice care. I can't say enough good things about the wonderful care and attention she received from hospice. They enabled her to stay in her own place until she took her very last breath, surrounded by the family she so loved.

Strength of the Sisterhood

Anita

One of the strengths of our family is our ability to recognize and support each other's needs. The sisters are all very different individuals, but together we are unstoppable.

Helen is very analytical, probably because she is a counselor. She looks at things realistically and rationally. The other side of Helen is creative; she loves to take pictures and then display them, and she is a wonderful dancer.

Ruth is compassionate, has a vibrant personality, and is very outgoing. She and my brother-in-law John run a successful jewelry business due, in part, to the fact that Ruth is wonderful at listening to people and making them feel special. When folks leave the jewelry store with the perfect gem for their wardrobe, they also feel like they are leaving with new friends.

The middle sister, Linda, is the quietest, but her gifts are her creativity and hospitality. She and her husband, Jim, live in a home that has a basement perfect for entertaining. All family gatherings are held at their home. No matter what the occasion, their home is always decorated perfectly. Whenever there is a project to be done that demands creativity, Linda is on speed dial.

Vicki is also creative, but in a different way. Having worked customer service for the news industry most of her career, she is good with people, has great organizational skills, and has a limitless energy for projects that she is passionate about. Like Vicki, I also have great organizational skills and an ability to see clearly what needs to be done. I oftentimes find myself volunteering to lead projects in my personal life because I am the one that likes to take charge.

These strengths have been repeated over and over again in our dealing with Mom and each other. When one of us has a need, the party line goes to work. A daughter would call Mom and mention that we had a problem, and soon all the other sisters knew and were ready to spring into action, offering advice, opinions, or aid. Some families might look at this as being busybodies, but in our family, it simply means that we have deep love for each other and are not afraid to show it.

As Mom aged, we all slipped into our roles. Even though Mom was able to take care of herself, she depended more and more on her girls. Ruth would call Mom every evening at exactly 9:00 p.m. so they could discuss world events or cry together over the evening's movie on the Hallmark Channel. Some nights, if the movie was running late, they would have to postpone their chat till 10:00 p.m.

Helen was in charge of calling Mom on the weekends, or once every six weeks she and her faithful dog, Emma, would make a weekend visit to Plum Landing. They were always a welcomed addition to Mom's home, and they also brightened the weekend of the other residents.

Vicki, Linda, and I were responsible for Mom's day-to-day needs. That ranged from grocery shopping to doctor appointments to balancing her checkbook and setting out her weekly pills. I had the ultimate responsibility for Mom's day-to-day affairs because I was the youngest and lived the closest, but I could not have done what was needed without Vicki and Linda. Together we made sure Mom was taken care of and also made sure we took care of each other so that we did not get stressed out and ignore our other professional and personal commitments.

Our biggest family challenge came in July of 2007. It was shaping up to be a warm but pleasant month. Our lives had all settled into a routine. Mom was happy at Plum Landing, all of us were healthy, and in the middle of our summer vacation activities, a huge tragedy hit the family.

My family was in Arkansas visiting Aunt Mildred and chillin' at Peals' Resort. Several of us had gone to town to get some snacks for the evening. We were on our way back, traveling cautiously down the winding roads with the sharp curves that have been carved into the rocky hillside. We were laughing about the afternoon activities at the pool and reminiscing about the week that was to end the next morning when our train of thought was shattered by the ringing of my cell phone. My daughter reached over to grab it, and it was Linda on the other end. When she found out I was driving, she said to call her as soon as we got to the resort. Already knowing that meant something was wrong, I drove a little faster to get back—I was sure something had happened to Mom.

We pulled into the driveway, and I was instantly dialing, my heart racing. Linda proceeded to explain that Mom was okay but our nephew Christopher had been found dead of a heroin overdose. Chris had been trying to overcome his addiction for the last ten years, and now, at the age of twenty-seven, he had lost the struggle. So many thoughts went through my mind. *How did this happen? Why? How is Vicki handling it?*

Holding back the tears because I loved this young man dearly, I asked Linda if we should come home immediately. She told me that Vicki had gotten a hold of Larry, who was in Canada on business, and he was heading home. Her daughter, Valerie, and her husband, Praveen, were already at the house. Their other son, Robb, was also there. She reminded me that we would all need to get our rest because we were in for a long and emotional journey. By the time I hung up the phone, the rest of my family had gathered around the picnic table I was slumped over. Huddled together, clinging to each other, we sobbed for a few moments before going our separate ways to individually process what had just happened.

I got in the car and drove to my prayer place. On the top of the Norfork Dam, there is a spot that overlooks the river and the entire valley. It is so peaceful, still, and awe-inspiring; I always feel the presence of God. Surrounded by the chirping of birds, I talked to my Lord. Chris had struggled with this addiction, but I knew he was a Christian, so that part of me was relieved. Finally, his battle was over, and he was at peace. But what about his loved ones? He had his parents, his sister and brother, a three-year-old daughter, Mom, the aunts, and all of his cousins. I prayed for strength and wisdom for all of us, and then I just sat silently.

After some time, I went back to the resort. By then everyone else had had their silent time, and we all drifted back together to tell our favorite Chris stories. Nobody slept well that night, hoping that this was all a nightmare, but in the morning, as we prepared to leave Arkansas, we all knew that reality would be awaiting us back in Illinois.

The next few days were filled with every emotion— joy that Chris was with Jesus and free from his earthly body and suffering, sadness for the family that would have to go on without him, and laughter as we shared the times we had spent with him.

The wake was held on the third day after his death. There was a horrible storm raging as people came to pay their respects to the family. An evening service was led by my niece's pastor who had met Christopher. He talked about the physical body and addiction and freedom in Christ. Next, there was a time for family and friends to speak. My daughter, Rebecca, was first to speak. She told how Chris, her older cousin by eight years, was always nice to her. When the other cousins who were twice her age picked on her, he was there to befriend her and play with her. Even when he was in his twenties, she always felt like he treated her with respect and paid attention to her. He had a kind heart, she concluded, and she would always remember him fondly.

Next came the stories from the rest of the aunts, uncles, and cousins. Chris was a good carpenter and was always there for family projects. He was good with his hands and helped on countless outdoor projects. He had a mischievous side and would love to play tricks on his sister, Valerie. He was a smart and a good student. He gave great hugs.

On and on the stories went—some we had all heard before but never tired of. There were also some new ones, but all of them celebrated the good in this young man and the part of him that we would all miss.

Finally, the evening was over, and only the immediate family was left to debrief on the day, sharing a few prayers and tears and hugs as we said good-bye till the next morning. Suddenly, lightning and thunder shook the entire building, causing the electricity to go out. We were standing in the middle of a funeral home in pitch darkness, which was an eerie sensation. The funeral director immediately started to light candles until we could see our way. After there was enough illumination to feel comfortable, Vicki told us this would have been Christopher's favorite part of the evening. How funny that he was able to play one last prank on us all.

Over the next months, Vicki would go through emotions that the rest of the sisters could not begin to understand. None of us were equipped to offer wisdom in this situation, so we stood by, making sure we were available to do anything we could to ease the pain.

At Chris's wake, a group of women from Hearts of Hope came to pay their condolences. They had met Vicki earlier when she had gone to their support group of families facing addiction issues. After the wake, Vicki reconnected with the group, and they provided both her and Larry a needed resource. These were others who had suffered through many of the same emotions and issues that Vicki had, and also some of them had lost a loved one to alcohol or drugs. The family came to know Lea Minalga, who was the founder of Hearts of Hope. She became an inspiration and a true friend.

In the spring of the next year, my daughters came to me with an idea. They wanted to do a walk and fundraiser in honor of Chris's memory. The walk would raise awareness of the issues of substance addictions, and the funds would go to help Hearts of Hope. Vicki and Larry agreed, and the whole family sprung into action to make this a reality.

The first Chris's Walk was held on the first anniversary weekend of Christopher's death. All the sisters, cousins, and many friends were there. It was an emotional weekend but also a positive one because his death would serve as a help to others. Now in our fourth year, Chris's Walk has raised over 15K to help with the cause. It is a testament to the strength and determination of my sister Vicki and the oneness of our family, along with the grace of God.

Vicki

Chris was my youngest son—a handsome, kindhearted son who had a heroin addiction. We had seen and been a part of his efforts over the past ten years in overcoming this drug and its hold on his life. There are those who will look upon this addiction as a weakness in Chris or poor parenting on the part of his family. I encourage you to refer to the resources at the end of this chapter to learn more about the *disease* of addiction, and I pray that your family is never affected by it.

It was July of 2007, and Chris had just recently been released from jail. I had taken a week's vacation time from work and was spending it with Caylee, his three-year-old daughter, so it was nice to include Chris in our activities. We took Caylee to the local parks, Chuck-E Cheese, Fourth of July Fireworks, the sprinkler park, and we just really had a good time together. Caylee had been staying with her grandparents in Eagerville, Illinois, and I would be driving her back at the end of the week. Chris was going to try to meet us that Sunday morning for the return trip if his painting job did not come through. It was just Caylee and me taking the drive, and Larry had left for Canada on business that same morning. Caylee and I chatted and snacked all the way there. She has always been a very loquacious child. We enjoyed our time together on the four-and-a-half-hour trip, singing, talking, and being silly together. I always missed Caylee on the ride home, as it was much quieter. Caylee was always so full of life, and she wore a smile that could warm you on the darkest day.

When I arrived home, the house was very still, and it was very hard to retire for the evening in the almost-eerie quiet. I put in a relaxation CD and tried to sleep. I guess I was overly tired, but sleep would not come. I was just starting to relax when a heard a knock on the front door. It was just after 11:00 p.m., and I wondered if it might be Chris.

As I looked out the front door, I saw two police officers. My mind immediately told me that Chris was in trouble, possibly jail; however, that was not the case. The officers proceeded to show me a picture and inquired if it was my son, Chris. I responded yes and asked if he was okay. They told me that he had died at approximately 9:00 p.m. that evening. I was numb. This was every parent's nightmare come true.

The officers stayed with me until I called my daughter, Val; son-in-law, Praveen; and my son Robb. Robb was the first to arrive because he lived only five minutes from my house. Val and Praveen lived forty-five minutes away. I was worried about Val; she and Chris had been so close, and I could hear the shock and sadness in her voice when I told her he was dead. She had also just recently shared with us that she was pregnant, and I feared she might miscarry from the stress of this event.

I called Larry. I hated to tell him that Chris was gone. He was so far away, and there was no one there to support him. Robb worked with him, and they were able to change his flight so that he would arrive the following day. I couldn't wait. This was a time when we really needed to be together.

Val and Praveen spent the night with me, and Praveen walked with me when I was too stir-crazy to sit anymore. We did our best to get some sleep in preparation for the days ahead. Early in the morning, I called Larry and we talked for hours, consoling each other from a distance.

The following day, Larry arrived home, and we started making the arrangements for visitation, funeral service, and burial. Everyone pitched in to help with the phone calls to the family. I was thankful that my sister Linda arrived, bringing a meal and just being there for me. We were looking through photos for the memorial boards that would be displayed at the funeral home. Chris was quite the character, and we found many amusing photos and memories that made us laugh and cry. Val would put the boards together the following day.

I remember one of the hardest things for Larry and me was to pick out the clothes that Chris would be buried in. He had very few possessions to his name, and that included clothing. Larry and I went to Kohl's and waited for the store to open, tears streaming down both our faces. I loved buying clothes for Chris on his birthday or for Christmas, but this was very different. The way he was dressed for this visitation would be engraved in my brain for the rest of my life—a burgundy shirt, black pants, belt, and socks.

The day came for the visitation, and all of my family was there, even my older sisters, who had very long commutes. At the start of the evening, the family was allowed to view Chris. This was the first time I would see him after his death and lying in his casket. Even in death he was handsome. I knew this was just his earthly body— that he was truly already gone to be with his Lord. He looked like he was just peacefully sleeping, except that his skin was hard to the touch. Still, I needed to have this final contact with him, to kiss his forehead, and to touch his closely shaved head. All of my family was also there, and we hugged and cried together.

When the visitation started and friends and family were arriving, I was kept busy greeting and talking to the guests. There was a steady stream, and the evening went quickly. I was overwhelmed with emotion at the wonderful stories that were reminisced about at the event. The music selection was perfect, and the officiating pastor who was well versed in addiction was wonderful, pointing out that everything said at that visitation stressed the importance of family to Chris as it did to all of us. Inside this funeral home, there were many tears shed; however, outside there was an out pouring of water also. A storm raged with lightning, heavy rain, thunder, and blustery winds.

It was approximately 9:00 p.m. when everyone had left, except the family, when the lights flickered and went out. As the funeral home director and staff scurried to light candles and flashlights, the family members, using their cell phones for light, approached the room with Chris's casket to retrieve their purses. I couldn't help but smile. I knew my mischievous Chris was having this last laugh on us.

The next day was the funeral and burial. Once again, after a beautiful service by our friend and officiator

Randy, numerous family members came forward, sharing stories of love, laughter, and just family. Oddly enough, I had never been to a visitation and funeral where so many memories of family and love were shared. Even though Chris was gone, I knew that his memory would live on forever with his family and friends. Little did I know how the death of this one young man would come to affect the lives of others for years to come.

In the days that followed, we tried to get our lives back together somewhat, although I knew it would never really be the same—we must go on. I was looking over the guest book and noticed that a couple of women from Hearts of Hope had come to Chris's visitation. I connected with Lea Minalga after a few days and told her that I wanted to work with Hearts of Hope. Too many of our children were dying from this disease of addiction, and we needed to do what we could to prevent more from dying.

Just prior to the first anniversary of Chris's death, Chris's Walk Against Substance Abuse was born. The event was only made possible by the hard work and support of our family and the grace of God. Every family member was involved, from donating raffle prizes to making monetary donations, spreading the word, making gift baskets, etc. It was a labor of love and unity, and it all started because of one man.

Yes, Chris was a heroin addict, but I will always be proud of him and how hard he struggled to be the best son, brother, and father that he could be. Because of him and, of course, God's direction, the family is now involved in jail ministry, and we will continue to do what we need to do to bring awareness of addiction to our communities.

I would like to share the following quote with you, in conclusion:

> You don't choose your family. They are God's
> gift to you, as you are to them.
>
> —Desmond Tutu

God has indeed given me the gift of family. My blessings abound.

Linda

During Mother's later years, she became more and more dependent on her daughters and sons-in-law. That's where the strength of the sisterhood came into play. Everyone stepped up to the plate, offering their assistance where needed.

Since Nita, Vicki, and I were all within several miles from Mom, we were the first string. Helen came several weekends to give us a much-needed respite, and Ruth would make her nightly calls, which provided us with our evenings to get caught up on our own responsibilities. All in all, Mother knew she was dearly loved and was never more than a phone call away if she needed us.

I never viewed Vicki as the strong one because she battled severe asthma from childhood through adulthood. When her son Chris passed away, she proved what a strong woman she truly was. Instead of burying herself in grief, she decided to turn Chris's death into an opportunity to help others who have or are in the midst of facing a loved one taken over by drug addiction. Vicki knew the sisters were available 24/7 if she needed us.

Two months after Chris's death, the sisters and Mother decided to go to Missouri to visit Ruth and John. We had the trip all planned, and then Vicki was notified that an inquest concerning Chris was going to be held on the day we were supposed to leave for Missouri. We decided to delay our trip by a few hours so we could all be at the inquest. We all prayed as Vicki took the stand and spoke before the jury, explaining why Chris's death had to be accidental. The jury ruled likewise. We then left the courthouse, picked up Mom, and took off for Missouri. The only sad part was that Nita couldn't be with us because her work couldn't get along without her.

Vicki drove, and I was the navigator. Mom and Helen offered their assistance from the backseat. At one point, Vicki thought she was an airline pilot as our car flew across a bridge!

My husband, Jim, and Vicki's husband, Larry, came several hours later after work. The plan was that the sisters were going to pick up Ruth and go to Branson while the sons-in-law were going to entertain Mom with niece Carla's help. Mother loved all the attention John, Jim, and Larry showered her. Carla took her to an afternoon tea and shopping.

We enjoyed our time together during this much-needed break from life. It was especially memorable because we all knew this would be Mother's last trip to Missouri.

Ruth

The last time I saw my nephew Chris alive was at his sister Valerie's wedding. We drove up to Illinois just that morning and arrived at the church only about half an hour before the service was to begin. Chris was standing out in front of the building and gave us a big smile as we approached him. I told him how handsome he looked as we exchanged hugs. His black hair was cut short in what I would call a crew cut. I remember patting his head and telling him that I liked his pokey-pokeys. Little did I realize that the next time I patted those pokey-pokeys, he would be lying in his coffin.

Although I probably knew Chris the least of all my sisters' children, I always felt a special connection to him, and I think he felt it too. I knew him as a sweet, kind, smiley, quiet boy. My photo albums hold mementos of just a snippet of his life: his annual school pictures, an occasional Christmas photo, a few thank you notes, and a letter he had to write and mail for penmanship class. There had been a few visits during the summers to our home in the Ozarks. I remember some picnics and that he loved fried chicken. I will never forget his big brown eyes and just how precious he was.

Chris's life was cut short because of some bad choices he made during his teen years that tormented him for the rest of his life. Due to his mother's vision, she has turned his death into victory so that others might not fall prey to the heinous addiction called drug abuse.

Chris's life cries out from the grave to those who would be attracted to a similar lifestyle. Who knows how many will turn from those things that would destroy their lives and bring them to that same fate? His mother has offered hope to all who would hear his story.

Helen

It's rather amazing that all five of us girls were born and raised in the same little house in Virgil. When we get together, we talk about our memories, and it's interesting how we recall things differently, but our values are very much the same. I love each and every one of my sisters and would trust them with my life. Throughout the years, I have come to know them more and appreciate their unique personalities.

My baby sister, Anita, has become quite a leader. She is a take-charge person, opinionated, and willing to stand up and work for her causes. She seems to always throw one more thing into her already-busy schedule. Just like the Energizer Bunny, she never stops. I didn't know Anita well when she was growing up because I was already gone from the home and was occupied with raising my own family. It seems there was a period when all the sisters were busy with our spouses and children. We still got together at Mom and Dad's, but not so much with each other. Mom was always the glue that kept us together and kept us informed about what each sister and their family was doing.

I so admire the strength of my sister Vicki. I'll never forget her composure when she spoke in front of the judge and jury at the inquest for her son Chris.

Chris died of an overdose of heroin. Vicki spoke on behalf of her son's honor and integrity. She needed for them to know that Chris would never deliberately take his precious life but that he finally lost his long battle over drug addiction. It took the jury but a few minutes to deliberate and come back with the verdict that his death was accidental. Vicki has since put purpose into Chris's death. She and Anita started the annual Chris's Walk to raise awareness of substance abuse issues. This year was the fourth annual walk, it's an event that all the sisters take part in to support Vicki, her family, and all the families who have been and are affected by drug abuse. One year, even though she was in a wheelchair, Mom also participated in the walk.

Linda, who was nicknamed "Dynamite" by our Uncle Mike, is just like that. She is little but very powerful in a subtle way. Linda seems to have acquired the perfect balance of activity and tranquility. I would say she has her priorities in order. Her home is the hub of most of the family get-togethers. She can entertain the entire family and make what would frazzle most to the max appear easy. Linda always takes time for her family. I frequently phone her because I can babble on and on, and she's such a good listener. I love to shop with Linda. She always knows where the bargains are, and she probably has some money-off coupons stashed away in the corner of her purse. Linda is probably the most sensitive of the sisters. She's not afraid to show her feelings. Linda gave freely of her time off from work to spend time with our mother. Mom would tell me how she looked forward to her Fridays with Linda.

Ruth wins the award for Miss Congeniality. When Ruth walks through the door, the place livens up. She could make a cigar-store Indian laugh with her witty stories. I would also give her the first place award for being such a great grandmother; in fact, her e-mail address has "Grammy" in it. That certainly speaks to the importance of that role in her life. Ruth and I clashed when we were teenagers. We had sort of a love-hate relationship. She would sneak into my closet and borrow my clothes and sometimes return them in well-worn shape. As I look back, she probably had to take them behind my back because I was too selfish to let her use them. However, at the same time, I was proud of her and even fixed her up with some of my ex-boyfriends.

I suppose I have some of those *firstborn* traits; I'm somewhat of a perfectionist (but only in some areas), I am very organized, make lots of lists, I'm logical, I put more pressure on myself than I do on others, I try to do it all, and I hate to be wrong. Now I know those things can be good or sometimes not so good. I also think the firstborn sometimes gets a bad rap. My sister Linda said it's my fault that she didn't learn to play the piano because I took lessons and didn't practice. Consequently, Mother said that she couldn't take lessons because she would be just like me and not practice. I also live a few hours away from the three younger sisters and sometimes feel disconnected— that's where Mom would come in. We used to talk every Saturday morning, and she would tell me what everyone was doing. I miss those chats, and for the longest time after she died, I would kind of expect to hear the phone ring and her voice saying, "Hello, Dear, it's just your mom."

I am a saver, another firstborn trait, so I record and save messages that are left on my phone. I have a recording of Mom singing "Happy Birthday" to me—how cute. When Mom was at Plum Landing, I would often pack up my dog, Emma, and spend the weekend with Mom. Those were good times—Emma was petted and pampered by the residents, and Mother and I had some wonderful chats. One evening we were talking about personal stuff, and I asked her who her favorite husband was. She quickly replied, "Your father, of course. He gave me you girls."

Even though this is the sisters' book, I think this would be a fitting place to stick in a bit about Mother's sons-in-law: John, Jim, Larry, and Jimmy. Mom loved these guys like they were her own flesh and blood. In fact, sometimes I think she would have taken their side instead of her daughters. They were always there to take her to doctor's appointments, move her belongings, share a lunch or dinner with her, do any repair work, and, of course, give their support to the Sisters.

The sisters were always there for Mom, each in our own special way. I think it's because we all knew that we were each so loved by her. I know in the future that love will continue to keep us together through all the ups and downs that life will bring to us.

Mom Leaves with Dignity and Grace

Anita

Shortly before her eighty-ninth birthday, Mom, because she was ill, was hospitalized. The diagnosis was congestive heart failure. Her heart was weak and not supplying the required circulation to her legs and feet, causing them to swell. Diuretics would help to keep the swelling down, but it would put a strain on her kidneys and potentially cause them to shut down. She would need to be closely monitored, but, according to the medical staff, it was only a matter of time until one of the organs no longer functioned.

We were in the middle of a February snowstorm. Vicki and Larry lived closest to the hospital, so it was decided that they would visit and the rest of us would stay home. When they arrived at the hospital, they were greeted by one of the doctors from the practice. The doctor suggested that we seek hospice care for Mom. It was a sleepless night for the sisters. Everyone received a call from Vicki, and we were faced with the realization that our mother was getting old.

The next day, the hospital arranged for us to interview several hospice organizations. Linda, Vicki, and I were to be in charge of making the decision with Mom. Helen and Ruth said they would trust our judgment. We all felt very relieved after meeting the representative from Seasons Hospice. They had a team that would take care of Mom. The nurse would come weekly or more often if needed. A hospice doctor was assigned to Mom, and he would visit as needed. There was a case coordinator who would oversee everything. She would help us tailor a plan that was suited for Mom.

Mom was back to Plum Landing the next day. Within hours, Seasons was on the premises. The case coordinator ordered a hospital bed because it would be easier for Mom to get in and out of and the railings would offer her needed support. Oxygen for the night and a portable unit for the days were brought in, just in case she needed them.

Next, Valerie, the nurse, came in. Upon meeting this bubbly, thirty-something woman, we knew Mom would be well attended to. Valerie checked Mom's heart, reviewed meds, and made her recommendations. She should come twice a week, she told the coordinator. There should also be music therapy provided, a social worker visit monthly, and a volunteer to just stop by and visit so Mom did not get lonely. Valerie suggested Mom should have someone older to talk to about life experiences and even about death.

Valerie next ordered all of Mom's medications to be sent directly to her apartment. They would arrive every other Friday via FedEx. If she felt Mom's medication should be adjusted, she would contact the doctor and have it changed and delivered. She reminded us that the balance between heart function and kidney function was crucial and that she was personally going to be responsible so Mom could function at the highest level possible for as long as possible. At any time we could contact Seasons with any questions or concerns.

One last suggestion came. They could bring in a CNA who would help Mom take her showers and get dressed in the mornings. Prior to that point, Mom was sitting in her chair, basking in all the attention, but someone helping her shower was not going to happen. She would never give up that privacy. At that point I realized Mom was not through fighting and she was "not going to go gently into that good night," as Dylan Thomas says in his poem by the same name.

Before Mom's arrival back home, it was suggested by Linda that we buy Mom some new bedding to make her hospital bed more attractive. A trip to Kohl's yielded purple sheets and a purple floral comforter with a matching pillow sham. Mom's favorite color was purple so it would provide her comfort as she drifted off to sleep. Once the bed arrived, brother-in-law Jim, ex-navy, came over to make the bed the proper way, complete with military corners. Next, Helen appeared with a giant stuffed purple cat to grace the bed when it was made. Everything looked perfect for our mom's first night of sleep in this next chapter of her long life.

Hospice is intended to make the last days of a loved one more comfortable, but in Mom's case, hospice made her life longer and fuller. Under the watchful care of Valerie, Mom gained back her strength and was able to proceed with her normal day-to-day activities. But the sisters could never get back to our normal routines. We were always on high alert when our phone rang. Calls to Mom were escalated, visits taken more often, and everything took on a higher meaning. We knew that sometime Mom would leave us.

A year later, we were preparing to celebrate Mom's ninetieth birthday. She had been sick a few weeks prior, and as we prepared the celebration, she joked with us, "What if I am not here for my birthday?"

Never wanting her to get the advantage, I replied, "We will just have the party without you. After all, the cake is ordered, and you know how much your daughters love sweets."

The event was to be held at Plum Landing. The building had a huge lunchroom, and they agreed to let us rent it after lunch on the Sunday before Mom's actual birth date. All the residents would be invited down to share cake, ice cream, and beverages with all of Mom's family and friends. Knowing in the back of our minds that this would probably be Mom's last birthday with us, we were determined to make it the best. People arrived the whole afternoon and lingered as long as possible, sharing with Mom this special day. By the end of the afternoon, Mom was visibly exhausted but glowing with happiness. She was wheeled up to her apartment and sat in her chair, where she spent the rest of the evening drifting in and out of sleep, not wanting to miss any of the chatter that was going on around her. It had been an incredible day and a wonderful tribute to a great woman.

A week later, Mom became very ill, and I took her to the doctor's office. He wanted to actually see her this time, not just change medicines over the phone. Her breathing was labored, and her legs were retaining large amounts of fluid. He took one look and sent her for blood work to confirm his suspicions that her kidneys had failed. When we arrived at the lab, it took all my power to get her inside. I presented the work order to the nurse, who showed me that the doctor had not signed it. They called his office, but he had already left, and his service could not locate him. We were told by the receptionist to wait until Monday and come back for the test then. I spent the night at Mom's house, not wanting to leave her alone.

The next day, her condition was worse, and we called Seasons. The nurse saw how fragile Mom had become and did not want her to get out of bed unless she felt strong enough. This meant putting a catheter in. I was given instructions on what to do and what signs to watch for. Determined I was not going to leave her apartment, I set up camp. My husband, Jim, brought over clothes, and soon I was joined by Linda and Vicki. They too knew we needed to be with Mom. Although Mom had recovered many times before, we knew these were her last days.

On Sunday she had completely stopped urinating, which was the sign that her kidneys had ceased to function. I called Ruth and then Helen. I could not guarantee them what lay ahead, but I felt certain they should come as soon as they could. Ruth became emotional and needed to hang up the phone and call me later. Helen had just returned from a two-week trip and would need to go to work a few days and get things settled. The doctor was going to check on Mom Monday morning, and after he left, I would apprise the sisters of the situation. Later that evening Ruth called back and said that her and John would be leaving early in the morning and would arrive by mid-afternoon.

On Sunday evening, Mom was strong enough to sit in her chair. We turned on a Hallmark movie but spent more time talking and laughing than actually watching the movie. Mom was visibly tired but did not want to go back to bed. She was enjoying listening to her silly girls, she said.

Monday morning, the doctor confirmed the worst. Yes, her kidneys had failed, and in less than a week, she would fade away. In the meantime, a hospice nurse would be stationed round the clock to aid us. The doctor also ordered a "pain kit" that could be used as needed. The kit contained something to lower Mom's heart rate, causing her breathing to become less labored and body to be less agitated. It also housed a vile of morphine to control the pain because her kidneys were not processing the toxins in her body.

Once we started administering the drugs, she would not be lucent, so we waited until they were really needed but didn't wait too long that it would cause Mom unnecessary pain. Mom was too weak to get out of bed at that point, so we all took turns spending time with her. Some of the moments were alone time, holding her hand

and talking or just sitting quietly. Other times many of us were in the room, savoring our time together with Mom.

Monday afternoon, there was a quiet time when Mom and I were alone. She needed to remind me of where all her financial items were, even though I already knew quite well. She had taken care of her finances impeccably over the years and wanted to make sure her beloved daughters had everything she owned. She reminded me that I was in charge of making sure everything was split equally, as she loved us all equally. I was also instructed to make sure that the daughters all remained close after she was not there to hold us together. After reminding her of the incredible job she did raising five smart, independent women, she was satisfied that her work was complete. She now voiced to me that she was tired and ready to go be with the Lord as soon as He was ready for her. I told her I would miss her but that she deserved to be with God. We would carry on without her, but she would always be in our hearts and minds.

Tuesday, Helen had changed her mind about working and was on the scene too. Plum Landing had an open apartment and let the sisters camp out there to catch up on some sleep or a shower. Between this and Linda's home, everyone was taken care of. Throughout the day Tuesday, friends, neighbors, and grandchildren came in and out of the apartment. Mom was alert and appreciative of the company. She was a very social person and valued her family and friends more than anything else. Before anyone went into the room, we explained what was going on but assured them that Mom wanted to see them. It was a special day for both Mom and the visitors.

Tuesday during the night, Mom's condition
deteriorated. Her breathing was labored, and she became
very agitated—I could see the pain. I knew it was time to
start administering the pain kit and call the doctor.

Wednesday morning brought sunshine and gentle
breezes. We opened the door to the balcony that was
off Mom's living room so that people could go out and
get some air and talk without disturbing Mom. Shelby,
Mom's music therapist, called and said he wanted to stop
by for a visit. Shelby had the voice of an angel, and Mom
adored him. When she heard Shelby's voice, you could
see Mom's whole body quiet, and then she would open
her eyes slightly. Shelby proceeded to play all of Mom's
favorites: "Eye on the Sparrow," "Amazing Grace," and
"When Irish Eyes Are Smiling." When he began singing,
"You Are my Sunshine," Helen and Ruth started singing
along. Being Christians, we knew that death was actually
a celebration of life and a joyous occasion as the person
prepared to join the Lord. Shelby always closed his
visits with Mom by singing his version of "Good Night,
Irene"—only he changed the name to Fran. He was not
sure if it was appropriate on this day, but I assured him
that it was what Mom and the family wanted. By the
time he finished, there was not a dry eye in the room,
including Shelby. He leaned over and gently kissed Mom
and told her that he loved her. I believe she said the same
to him.

When he left, the chaplain from Seasons arrived to
pray with the family. Brother-in-law John had already
anointed Mom with oil, and we had all prayed earlier,
but it was wonderful for the chaplain to comfort us

also. Next, the doctor arrived. After examining Mom, he concluded that she was nearing the end, but it was not imminent that day. I should continue on with the medicines as often as needed to keep Mom comfortable.

Upon hearing the prognosis, everyone decided to go for a walk. Vicki; her daughter, Valerie; and I remained. We were not about to leave Mom's apartment. Moments after everyone left, with the apartment quiet, I walked into Mom's room to sit by her side. The moment I stepped into the room, she took one last breath and was no longer in her earthly body. Valerie walked in shortly after, and I motioned for her to get Vicki. The three of us hugged each other, tears streaming down our faces. Then we took turns saying good-bye to Mom before we were whisked out of the room by the hospice nurse, who needed to make some preparations to the body and call the doctor with the time of death.

We went into the other room and began calling the cell phones of the other sisters. By the time they arrived back, the body was ready for viewing, and the funeral director was on his way. Ironically, it was the week before Easter, the same week that Dad had died so many years earlier. Mother's last days had been with the same grace and dignity with which she had lived her whole life.

Vicki

Mom, when did you get old? When did your body start to fail? I never noticed. I guess as I began to age, I didn't realize that you were aging too. My mother, who was always there for me, always supportive, always loving, always wanting only the best for me.

At the age of nine, I was diagnosed with asthma. This was not uncommon, as asthma and other lung conditions were prevalent on both sides of our family; however, it did put some limitations on my life as a child. I could not be as active as my sisters, and I was prone to ear infections, pneumonia, and bouts of asthma. I remember the numerous trips to the doctor and even rides in the ambulance from Virgil to get me to the hospital in a timely fashion for respiratory treatments and hospitalization, but what I remember the most about this time of my life was the constant care of my mother. She seemed tireless as she sat up with me into the wee hours of the morning, rubbing my back to help me relax and breathe better. We got an air conditioner to help with the summer allergies. We took a vacation to try another climate. She took me for allergy shots. All this extra care and cost she provided so easily, never playing the martyr as I might have. Up until the day my mother passed away, she would inquire if I was wearing my jacket when it was cool in the morning or if I was getting enough sleep or if I was taking my medicine (something that we had to constantly be on her about the last years of her life).

Even at the age of fifty-five, Mom still made sure to let me know that she was still my mom and made sure I was okay. Mom had the biggest, caring heart, and she has passed that trait down to each and every one of her girls. We are truly blessed to be Fran's daughters. Even as I write this, I can still sense mom's love enveloping my life as it brings back warm, comfortable memories of this caring woman.

Mom had always been an independent woman. She pretty much knew what she wanted and how to get it. When she had something set in her mind, she would achieve it, although I know she never took any classes on goal-setting, five-year plans, etc.—she didn't need them. As Mom began to age, she made it clear that she never wanted to go to a nursing home, and of course, we would do all that we could to keep her comfortable in her own home. Wouldn't I want it the same way? So when she became ill, we gathered our family and put together schedules for Mom's care. The word *hospice* was new to us, and we would find that it was not only for the care of the ill person but also for the support of the family. While the family could go about their daily business, hospice would tend to Mom, giving us the comfort in knowing that she was being taken care of. From daily nurse visits, music therapy, and conversation, hospice made Mom happy and comfortable, and her life was prolonged an additional two years under hospice care. We became quick friends with the Seasons staff, and to this day they hold a warm place in our hearts.

I will always remember these final days that I was able to spend with Mom, cherishing the overnights that I spent and the talks that we had together. Mom was preparing us for her death. She knew that these would be her final days, and she was ready to go. She had been fighting for so long, and she was ready to join her Maker and Dad in heaven. I asked her to give

Chris a big hug for me too, and she said she would. She missed him too. Oh, how her heart hurt when she had to see a grandson pass away. Family meant so much to Mom, and she has instilled that into each of her children. We will pass it down to ours, and Mom's wisdom will continue through the generations.

After Mom's passing, the funeral home director came to transport her body for preparation for a visitation and burial. This may seem morbid to some, but we had been prepared for Mom's death and had already lived through the death of Dad and Chris. We were allowed to remain in the room as the funeral home director carefully got mother onto the gurney. He treated her as he would his own mother, with care and dignity. Then he asked us if we wanted to tuck her in and say our last good-byes. We were appreciative that we could tend to Mother for the last time and give her a final kiss good-bye. She would have been proud of us, but she always was proud of us. We could do no wrong in Mother's eyes. She adored each and every one of us, and she always made sure that we knew that and that she treated us each the same. The only thing she asked of us was that we didn't fight over any of her things, which I assured her we would not. Mother was so prepared for her death that she, of course, had a headstone and burial plot next to Dad's, plus she had chosen what she wanted written in her funeral card and the song she wanted played at her funeral. We girls worked with the funeral home prior to her passing, selecting a casket with flowers adorning the corners. We, of course, showed it to her, and she was pleased.

Things didn't go quite so smoothly, though. The day of Mother's visitation, Nita received a call from the cemetery. It seemed there was a new law that required us to view the grave prior to the burial. I just happened to be with Nita as we were shopping for new shoes for the visitation. We called my husband, Larry, and all three headed out to Virgil a little in awe of the day's proceedings. We got to Virgil and were told that there wasn't enough room for Mom's casket next to Dad's, but it was not uncommon for one casket to be laid atop another. With no other choice, we moved forward with that, this whole day being a little on the weird side and the visitation just hours away. Things progressed in a normal fashion from there with a beautiful visitation and the burial.

The first year without Mom was not easy, the first holiday being Mother's Day. I used to call Mom every morning. I miss talking to her. Birthdays came, Thanksgiving, and Christmas—it just was not the same without Mom. Things will forever be changed.

Linda

Mother was visibly getting weaker and weaker before our very eyes. She was not sure she would make it to her ninetieth birthday party. We put her in charge of the guest list and encouraged her to phone her friends and relatives with a personal invitation. This gave her an opportunity to chat with people, and it also helped get her mind on something other than her failing health. The party was a huge success and was well attended.

A couple of weeks later, we knew Mother would be leaving us soon. Her health was deteriorating rapidly. This was a difficult time for us, and we spent as much time with Mom as we could. Nita, Vicki, and I worked out a schedule so someone was with Mom at all times. I try to erase the images of Mother's last days from my memory—they are too painful to relive.

Mother's memorial service was quite a tribute to a wonderful woman's life. There were tables displaying pictures and memorabilia of Mother's lifelong journey. Whenever I hear "On Eagles Wings," "Amazing Grace," "I Can Only Imagine," and "I Will Rise," my mind drifts back to that sad but glorious day when Mother went home to meet her Savior. Whenever I start to feel sad about mother being gone, I refer to the poem she picked out to be put on her memorial folder: "A Mother's Farewell to Her Children."

Thanks, Mom, for giving me such a good example on how to be a good person, mother, wife, and grandmother!

Ruth

How quickly a lifetime passes. Psalm 103:15-16 says, "As for man, his days are like grass, he flourishes like a flower of the field; the wind blows over it and it is gone, and its place remembers it no more."

Mom's ninetieth birthday was a momentous occasion for all of us. John and I closed our business to enable our entire family to attend her party. We knew that this might be her last birthday celebration. When we saw her fragile little body, the reality of it finally hit each one of us. My mother had become weak and frail. In my heart I knew that she wouldn't be with us too much longer.

We stayed an extra day and then headed back home, where Mom and I continued our evening phone conversations. Sometimes she was too exhausted to talk for very long, and other nights she chatted on but in a weak voice.

A few weeks before she passed away, she told me about an unusual reoccurring dream she had been having about our Dad. In her dream, Dad appeared to her and told her that he would see her soon and that they would again be together. Mom related to me that she never had dreams about Dad, and thus, she found this very puzzling.

"What do you think it means?" I asked. Mom said she didn't know, but in my heart I felt I understood.

One day in March, that phone call I so dreaded came—Mom was dying. John and I were once again making a trip to Illinois to spend Mom's last days with her. On our way up this time, we saw nothing but barren ground and naked trees—a sad reminder of how quickly the seasons of life pass. But those who belong to God will enter a season that is unending and eternal. Looking out the window at this sparse scene, we realized that what we were viewing was only temporary and that, once again, it would come into its full glory—a glory that only God can bring forth in the lives of those he calls.

During this journey, we reflected on what an amazing woman my Mom was. She was more than just a loving mother and grandmother, she was a caring neighbor and devoted friend, a good cook, and an accomplished seamstress. She was a memory maker who created many treasured times for her family and friends. She was a teacher and mentor. We learned how to be confident women and homemakers by her example. Because she was kind and caring to everyone, we emulated these traits, and they helped us form our personalities and characters. We are honored to have been able to sit under her tutelage . She truly does live on through the members of her family. Sometimes I catch a glimpse of her when I glance in the mirror or when I hear myself use the exact words or expressions she would use. I'm not the first one in my family to cry giant crocodile tears during a Hallmark movie. *Andy Griffith*, *Little House on the Prairie*, and *Christy* are still some of my favorite programs, just as they were Moms.

Mom's death was a beautiful thing. She was in her own apartment, lovingly surrounded by her daughters and their husbands. Some years back, Jim Tarmichael, her son-in-law, had led her to the Lord, and she had made a confession of faith. Because she had never been baptized, Jim asked her if she would like to do that while we were there with her. She said yes, so Jim baptized her right there in her bed, using a glass of water from her nightstand. Mom had such an incredible spirit of peace. Some of us sensed the presence of angels at her bedside.

Because our hope is in the Lord, we believe in a more glorious day in his presence where there will be no more pain or suffering. We rejoice in the fact that one day we will be reunited with our mother for eternity.

Helen

I had never seen anyone die before, much less my own mother, so I have nothing to compare the experience to. During her last hours, her breathing was labored, and it had a raspy sound, but she appeared to be in a peaceful state. Occasionally, she would flutter her eyelids as we would take our turns holding her hand and talking to her. This told us she did indeed realize that we were with her.

I prefer to remember my mother's spirit, her zany personality, and her love of life. All of us will someday have the experience of our bodies growing old and the decline of our functioning, but our spirit always remains with all of those we leave behind.

Mother was a spiritual person, but not one who would push her beliefs on others or judge them. She attended church regularly, and when she lived at Plum Landing, she worshiped in their chapel with the other residents. Occasionally, on the weekends while I was visiting, she would suggest we watch Joel Osteen on TV instead of going to the chapel. It was getting increasingly difficult for her to walk and get around. One morning after Pastor Osteen's program, we were discussing his message and how we understood it. Mother voiced her opinion and then added, "And he's cute too."

Mother was very practical and organized—she had her funeral planned. She was able to talk about her impending death with us girls. As I look back at those times, I kind of think those serious conversations were more difficult for the sisters than for Mom. I recall one evening she brought out a little book of poems and asked me if I would copy one by Helen Steiner Rice titled "A Mother's Farewell to Her Children." She said she wanted it on her funeral remembrance card because it expressed exactly how she felt.

The days, weeks, and months after her death, I would sometimes have a moment or two when I still couldn't believe she was gone. I would want to pick up the phone and call her or think of something I wanted to ask or tell her. Even now I constantly think of her sayings. Once in a while, one of her favorite phrases comes out of my mouth, and I have to smile. She would teasingly call us "slave drivers" when we urged her to exercise or do something that she found unappealing. She got that funny little smile on her face and would sometimes make a silly remark just to see our reaction.

I often look through my many photo albums and relive the fun times my sisters and I had with her. There are photos of her at weddings, showers, picnics, family reunions, birthdays, baptisms, First Communions, and all sorts of events. She was always willing to pose for a photo, especially if she had a new outfit. I love the silly photo of her and me pretending to be in a photo booth, or the one of her with a sweatband around her head and a ping-pong paddle in her hand, or the one of the Chris' Walk with Jim pushing her wheelchair, or the one of her holding the great-grandkids, or the one of her laughing at the phony voice coming from the outdoor toilet—the list goes on and on. She was such a great sport. It's all about living life to the fullest. That's the legacy left by our Mom.

Sisters Still Doing Our Thing

Anita

*A*fter Mom died, the sisters vowed we would stay together. We had become so close over the last few years and truly enjoyed each other. Mom left us all some money, and we started planning on taking a sisters' vacation. I wanted Europe, but several of the husbands did not want five females traveling alone across the pond. Vicki finally came up with the perfect solution. She and Larry owned several weeks at a timeshare, and they could book a week in Cabo San Lucas, Mexico. It would be a three-bedroom villa that would sleep ten, the exact number we needed if all the sisters and spouses were to go. The trip was booked for May 7, 2011, almost a year away.

In the meantime, there were plenty of other family gatherings that needed the attention of the sisters. After Mom's death, there were papers that needed to be signed by all of us. Plans were made to all get together in May, a month after her passing, to sign the papers, take a day trip to Chicago's Lincoln Park Zoo, and the next day all participate in a 5K charity walk to benefit the local food pantry. As the tour guide for the Chicago trip, it was my duty to make sure everyone got to the train station on time and that we connected in Chicago with the right buses and that nobody got separated from the herd. Although keeping this group together was never an easy task, we made it safely to and from Chicago. At every junction along the way, people would comment to us about our group. What fun we were having, and all being sisters. They were amazed that we got along so well and wished they had the same relationship with their siblings.

The next day, the 5K was amazing. Helen, the oldest, was still the best athlete. She crossed the finish line, winning the gold medal for fastest female in her age group. Her boyfriend, Terry, not to be outdone, also won a gold medal for the best male in his age group. The rest of us were happy to cross the finish line on our own accord. Once again, all the other participants were surprised that this huge noisy group that was having so much fun together was a family of five sisters and their spouses. Many of them commented on how jealous they were of the relationship. They longed to have a close relationship with their own siblings. We were always quick to tell them they could be part of this family if they wanted. The more the merrier.

In July we were all together again because of the third annual Chris's Walk. Every one of the sisters played an important role. Helen took pictures, Ruth and Linda worked the raffle and silent auction tables, and I was the MC. Vicki, of course, was one of the speakers, and she also greeted all of the participants. After the walk, we all went back to Linda's house, where Jim made burgers, and we all sat around, exhausted from the day but enjoying each other's company and support.

As fall and winter came, we did not see each other but still remained in touch via e-mail and phone calls. Word came that Ruth's daughter, Carla, was directing a play that her son, Chase, and some friends had written. It immediately went on our calendars as a "Must-Do Weekend in Missouri." The play was titled *Distorted Perceptions* and was set in a senior living community called Plum Landing. Chase had always held a special spot in Mom's heart, and we were all thrilled that he was thinking about her. This play was the annual production of the Home School Association and the highlight of the year, showcasing the creativity and passion of the students. The pressure was on Carla and Chase as they worked the winter months into the spring perfecting their work.

Now only three weeks before our Cabo trip, Linda and Jim, Vicki and Larry, and I all took the Friday off work so we could arrive in time for the evening presentation. What an amazing event the play was. The script had a strong plot and several subplots that kept you entertained and on the edge of your seat the entire two hours. The actors and actresses, most of whom had taken improv classes from Carla, played their characters with such precision that I truly felt like I was watching senior citizens. When the final curtain call was over, it was announced that the play was going to be published by a local publishing house. The aunts were swelling with pride and so thankful that we could be on hand to share in this event.

Finally, the Cabo trip was upon us. The limo was scheduled to be at Linda's at 3:30 a.m. for our 8:00 a.m. flight. Nine of us boarded the limo—Ruth and John; Linda and Jim; Vicki and Larry; Helen and her boyfriend, Terry; and me. My husband, who did not want to go to Mexico and had just spent his two weeks of vacation on the family farm in Arkansas, snapped a picture, and after kisses and hugs, we said our good-bye for a week.

The flight to Mexico was uneventful. I enjoyed flying as a way to catch up on my reading. I liked to be alone, so I sat near the front of the plane while all the rest of the family sat together in two rows toward the back of the plane. Every now and again, I could hear the loud voices and laughing, so I knew they were back there enjoying themselves also.

When the plane landed in Cabo, we were immediately greeted by the warm breezes and the strong rays of the sun. The ninety-degree temperature was welcoming; it was in the forties when we left Chicago. After clearing customs and dodging all the locals trying to sell us wares, we got our transportation to the Hacienda Del Mar. Pulling into the resort, we realized this was not going to be our normal vacation. Lush greens and perfectly groomed palm trees lined the paths, and every tropical blooming flower could be observed. Bellmen in crisp linen shirts met us and secured our luggage. We were welcomed by a resort representative who gave us fruit and beverages to refresh us and explained the resort layout before we were taken to our villa.

The villa had three bedrooms. The master suite would be Vicki and Larry's, since it was their timeshare. The other two bedrooms both had two queen-sized beds and a private bathroom. Everybody staked out their territory and began to put their possessions away. Linda, Jim, and I were going to be roommates, and Ruth, John, Helen, and Terry would occupy the other room.

As the week went on, we settled into a routine, learning quickly who snored, who took the longest in the bathroom, and who always left a mess. We never got in a fight, but there was some lighthearted ribbing.

Sunday, our first full day at Cabo, we realized we needed to go to town and get some rations. Food at the resort was expensive, and we wanted to save as much as possible for souvenirs and other activities. We all piled into a taxi and headed for downtown Cabo San Lucas. First stop was lunch. Some of us wanted local fare, so we ate at an open-air restaurant called La Quesadilla. We had authentic Mexican cuisine and were serenaded by a strolling guitarist. At one point, some salsa music came over the speaker system, and Helen and Terry treated us and the rest of the patrons to some of their own Mexican-style salsa dancing. Meanwhile, across the street, the less adventurous part of the group was dining at Burger King. Later that evening, Jim got sick, and we all were sure it was from the American food.

Next, we went to the flea markets that dotted downtown. Bargaining was part of the charm of buying the brightly colored sundresses for our grandchildren. I spotted a Green Bay Packers poncho that I knew I must have as a souvenir for my hubby, Jim. Wanting to just purchase it at the first store, I mustered up all my willpower and haggled, acting as if I didn't even care about the item. I walked away from three vendors until finally I reached the best deal of the day. Relieved, I put it in my bag and did not let it leave my clutches again until I reached the villa where I could pack it away in my suitcase.

As the bright sun shone down on our fair white complexions, it became obvious that sunhats would be a required item. Helen, Ruth, and I all purchased the same design of hat, just in different colors. By purchasing in bulk, we knew we would get a better deal from the charming young Mexican lad who was showing us his selection.

Of course, every memory along the way, and every storekeeper with which we made a deal, was immortalized with pictures taken by Helen, Linda, and Vicki. I took my camera with me, but I soon realized I was wasting my time trying to compete with the "photo wizards."

On Monday, Helen, Terry, Ruth, and John all signed up to do a timeshare presentation in exchange for some discount coupons and some free meals. The rest of us were not about to give up a precious morning to do this. Instead, we decided that we would test the water aerobics class that was being held every morning at 10:00 a.m. We arrived at the class and joined a few other women. The girl who led the aerobics was a petite young thing with a charming Spanish accent.

She did all of her counting in Spanish, which didn't fool us. We still knew we were repeating the same move over and over until we reached eight, and then the same number of repetitions as she counted backward in Spanish to *uno*. But after every exercise, no matter how badly we had done, she always said, "Perfect," so we felt good and were inspired to continue onward.

When Helen and Ruth arrived back from their timeshare presentation, they were envious of our adventure and vowed to go to aerobics the next morning. This activity became one of our favorite trip memories. Every day as the sisters and their husbands arrived, more and more of the other guests joined us. By the end of the stay, we had made quite a number of pool buddies, all of who knew we were the sisters from Illinois and many of them envious of the exciting adventure we were having.

On Friday, it was the instructor Pamela's twenty-second birthday, and we all sang Happy Birthday and gave her a cake made out of Twinkies and a card signed by all the aerobic participants. She said she was genuinely touched by the gesture and told us all that we were her best group ever. This might have been equivalent to her saying, "Perfect," after every exercise, but it made us feel good anyway.

During the week, we went to a glass factory, ate at several amazing restaurants, and went on a glass-bottom boat, where we saw all varieties of saltwater fish and seals. We also did lots of sun tanning and swimming in the five pools at the resort, but the best part of the week was just spending time with the family.

One week and six hundred pictures later, we were back in Chicago, safe from this adventure. I can't predict what lay in store next for the sisters, but whatever it is, we will be doing it together.

Vicki

I have been blessed to have four sisters—the fifth, Loretta, I would never know, as she passed away as an infant. People hearing that there are five of us are somewhat amazed and even envious. We all get along well. I can't say we haven't had a misunderstanding or two, but we have worked through them. There have been some people who have felt bad for our dad, that he had never had a son, but we were not prissy girls. Dad taught us how to check our oil, put gas in our cars, put air in our tires, use a hammer and other tools, and many other things. We were his girls, and there were no regrets.

My oldest sister, Helen, is creative, beautiful, a counselor, and a wonderful dancer. She is the sister I know the least because she had already moved away from home when I was growing up. I have some great memories of overnight stays at her house, though, and her children are only slightly younger than me. She also is the one who gave me the worst haircut in my entire life, and on my golden birthday! But I forgive her. I just won't let her near me with anything sharp. I am proud of Helen because she got her degree later in life. She's a wonderful mother and grandmother, and she truly enjoys life.

Ruth is the second oldest, and I was allowed to go on dates with her and John when I was growing up. She is also the sister that was the worst cook, dreaming up concoctions like lentil burgers, mock apple pie—made entirely of Ritz crackers—etc. Mom would let her cook, and we were forced to try her dishes. Oh, and don't forget the eggnog—I never have. Yuck! She also is the sister who would have us over on weekends, and we had to clean up her dirty, crusty dishes. I have always felt a special closeness with Ruth, though, and I love visiting her and John at their home in Osage Beach. She is a kind, loving person. I remember many crazy meals at her home, where we had to dress to a theme (i.e., Chinese night). Ruth and John also own KK Jewelers in Missouri, and like Mom, I love jewelry.

Linda, even though she was terribly mean as a child, has grown into a caring person. She loves to decorate and entertain. She also has a creative side to her, and she has created many gift baskets for Chris's Walk and other occasions. We have spent many a wonderful time shopping together.

Nita is the sister who is closest to me. We are four years apart in age, and our children are close in age. We have been through many things together and at one time even lived together. When I was having my first child, Valerie, Nita was filling in on my job for me. I remember training her over the phone from my hospital bed because that was her first day, and Valerie came early. Together, every year, we work hard to put on Chris's Walk Against Substance Abuse. We minister in two jails together, educating, providing reading material, praying, and listening. There is nothing that we cannot accomplish together; we are pretty much of the same mind on things.

There is an occasional time when I need to reel her back in because she is over the top, but that's what I do. She is quick to remind all of us that she is the only one in our family who is a kindergarten graduate. Yeah, whatever.

So these are my sisters. Each has their own personality and things they are good at. When we are together, it is great fun. When we are apart, we still hold each other in our hearts. None of my sisters are judgmental, and each one is caring, just like Mom wanted them to be. People who see us together are envious because we all do get along. I feel terrible when I hear others say that they haven't spoken to their siblings in ten years, or whatever the case might be. I would hate that. There is nothing that could keep me from talking to and being with my sisters. My wish for everyone is to have the kind of relationship that we sisters have. Each year it just gets better. Thanks for my sisters, Mom.

Linda

Our Cabo adventure definitely brought out our unique personalities.

Helen is adventurous—she's always taking a class, going to some seminar, or attending an event where she is the self-appointed photographer. She is also an excellent listener. On vacation, she never missed a photo op.

Ruth is the humorous one. She always has some interesting story to tell about her dogs, John, or her grandkids. She also seems to be the most impulsive and gullible one. Oh, did I mention she is the only blonde-headed sister? Ruth is the sister who jokingly said we should write a book.

Anita, who is the mover and shaker in the group, heard about Ruth's idea and literally ran with it. If you want something done, tell Nita about it, but if you're not serious about it, keep quiet around Nita. I wouldn't be surprised if Nita enters the political arena in the near future. Like I said, she can make things happen! Nita has taken on the role of keeping the family together. She always calls to check on what has been happening and proceeds to share what is going on in the other sisters' lives. The grapevine lives on.

Vicki is Nita's right-hand gal. They act as a tag team and convince you to do things that are way out of your comfort zone. Vicki has unlimited energy and enjoys planning our trips. I wonder what she'll come up with next. She's involved in several prison ministries and is always looking for new ways to serve.

That leaves me. I'm more of an introvert and am pretty content with taking care of my husband, grandkids, and house. I do enjoy decorating and have an awesome napkin ring collection. Writing this book has been difficult for me. I'm not good at sharing my thoughts and feelings with the entire world and doubt that many people would find them that interesting. Since I'm afraid of the tag team, Nita and Vicki, I had no choice but to complete my writing assignment.

Ruth

Whether we are vacationing in Cabo San Lucas; touring the Jelly Belly Factory in Wisconsin ; laughing it up at Silver Dollar City in Branson, Missouri; meeting early in the morning for breakfast at Denny's; or enjoying a cookout at Linda and Jim's house, it is always a joy to be in my sisters' company. My husband jokingly says, "I wish I was a sister."

Although I have spent most of my adult life in Missouri and not near my sisters, we still have a bond that time and distance can never break. My sisters are my dearest friends. As we get older, we realize more and more just how precious our relationship is and how blessed we are to have each other!

Helen

The beauty of being a sister is that when you connect with the people you grew up with, you can go back and be a kid again. You can laugh and giggle and just be crazy. You don't have to be a dignified, responsible person because a sister knows who you really are. You can be goofy, tearful, or whiney and they still love you. Amazing! That's why we're all able to spend time together and not end up scratching out each other's eyes.

We all have our own little weird ways, but those oddities are accepted by the flock. I could go on and name a few of those quirks, but that would be pushing my luck.

A Tale of Five Sisters

How fortunate I am to have four sisters, because sometimes I get lonesome and need to talk to family. You know how frustrating it is to call, hoping to chat, only to find the person is not available? Well, I have four chances that someone will be there for me.

Family was extremely important to Mother. In fact, she was instrumental in keeping her other two husbands connected with their children. So that's one more reason for us sisters to remain close—it pleases our Mom. We have always done things together, but our mother was usually at the hub of the activity.

The year after Mom died, the sisters and their spouses took a vacation to Cabo San Lucas, Mexico. We had a delightful time, and we knew Mother would be so happy to see us all together. We purchased a ceramic cross made in Mexico to take back for Mom's gravesite. Her spirit is still with us, and she's probably wondering where "her girls" will be traveling on their next adventure.

Conclusion

*W*e hope you enjoyed the book and have been entertained.

We grew up in a close-knit community, in a very loving family. Our parents instilled high values in us that have served us well in our lives.

But we realize the world has changed since the five of us grew up. Family values have changed, and it is difficult to find a family as close as ours.

- The divorce rate is over 40 percent.

- The poverty level is at an all-time high of over 46 million (*NY Times*).

- Children living in a single-parent home are the norm.

- Some 33,000 violent street gangs, motorcycle gangs, and prison gangs with about 1.4 million members are criminally active in the United States today (FBI source).

- In 2007, suicide was the tenth-leading cause of death in the United States, accounting for 34,598 deaths (National Institute of Mental Health).

This makes it so very important to treasure the relationships family provides and to work diligently to remain close to whatever family structure you do have. It is important to forgive and forget the shortcomings in each other and to love and celebrate the unique contributions of each member.

> Be devoted to one another in love. Honor one another above yourselves.
>
> Romans 12:10 (NIV)

God bless you and may He keep your families safe, healthy, and happy.

—The Sisters

Appendix

Mom's Stories

*C*hristmas was always important to Mom. Every year her daughters and grandchildren received a card and some money. She also would make an endless variety of Christmas cookies, and every family got a tin of them. Her last few years did not allow her to do all that baking, so with a little encouragement from her daughters, she wrote us a story instead.

Mom only had an eighth-grade education, but she was a wonderful writer, never needing spell check. We hope these bring as much joy to you as they do to us.

—The Sisters

Christmas 2006

A special tribute to my precious girls, who have brought great joy into my life.

It all began a number of years ago when I first got married to George Altepeter. A year later, Helen was

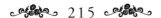

born—a beautiful, bouncy, black-haired girl who was always around to help me.

Three years later, Ruth came along. She could always keep me on my toes. She loves to talk with me on the phone for hours, giving me advice, even though I don't always take it.

Linda came a little later. She seemed to be the shy one in the family, but she could get your attention, especially when she just wanted to fight with Vicki. But Linda is always there when I need her and gives me lots of encouragement when I need it.

Next was Vicki, who is my best shopper. I believe she would drive to Chicago if I needed just one thing that she couldn't find here. Thank you.

Last but not least, Anita, my youngest, who is my secretary, handyman, checkbook balancer, and all those good things.

And now on to my grandchildren and great-grandchildren—all of you.

A special welcome to the newlyweds: Ben and Heather, Trina and Mark, and Valerie and Praveen.

Jacob is a little charmer, and with Kerry, they make a handsome couple.

An award goes to Sarah for being so full of energy to raise Bethany and Jeremy. I praise you for all good work. Love you, my dear.

What do you know? Becky is an honor student and president of the National Honor Society at her school. She is a cheerleader, in the band, plays soccer, and has received many awards. She gets an extra medal for working hard to achieve her goals.

Chris, thank you for getting me moved to North Aurora and all your hard work. And I can't forget little Caylee, who is bringing up the rear. Congratulations to her proud grandparents, Vicki and Larry. She's quite the little gal.

I better not forget my four sons-in-law: John, Jim T., Jim L., and Larry. They have been there whenever I needed anything, from being a painter to cleaning the yard and all those good jobs. A medal with extra gold stars is awarded to you for chauffeuring me around and for all the times you have been there to encourage me. You are so special to me. I love you and thank you.

To Gretchen and Tom, Kelly and Kris, Michelle and Michael, Vanessa and Tim, Carla and Bruce, and Eric and all your children. Even though I don't see you very often, I am proud of all of you and love the pictures and stories of your families.

I hope I am not forgetting anyone, because it sure was not intentional. I thank you all for everything good in my life. May you all have a blessed holiday.

All my love,
Mom

Mom's Letter, Written on August 2, 2007

I was born on March 16, 1920. My parents were John Schmitt and Margaret Loerzel. I was the third oldest of a family of twelve. My brothers and sisters were Katherine,

Elizabeth, Frances (me), Loretta, Louis, Ralph, Esther, Jean, Margaret, Nicholas, John, and Robert.

I was born in Aurora, Illinois, but we moved to Virgil because of my dad's health. We lived on a farm where we had lots of cows, pigs, chickens, and a big garden. We lived on the same farm for about sixteen years and then moved to the farm that William Schramer owned. I was married by that time, so I didn't move there.

We all went to St. Peter and Paul School in Virgil. We had a busy life going to school and working on the farm. We all had jobs to do after school. Loretta and Louis helped with the milking and the barn chores. My job was to take care of the chickens and pick up the eggs. We always had chicken lice, and I hated cleaning out the nests. Then we helped with supper and the dirty dishes. We all learned to cook and sew at an early age. Mother was a really good seamstress and was always altering someone's clothes to fit the next one in line. We always had hand-me-downs—we hardly ever had new clothes. Mother was always making dresses for school.

I remember having two dresses for school, so we didn't change clothes every day; some were made from feedbags. Remember, we didn't have jeans, so we wore dresses to school all the time—no sleeveless dresses, and they had to be no shorter than to our knees with long stockings and high boots in the winter.

We always walked to school unless it was extremely cold, and then Dad would pick us up. I drove the tractor for baling hay because it took four of us to do the job. I also helped Dad pick corn in the fall. We didn't have a picker, so we walked between the rows and picked the ears from the stalks. It was hard work, and I got really tired by the end of the day. We had about an acre of garden that kept us all busy weeding and picking vegetables. My mother and dad made fifty gallons of sauerkraut every fall. It was a big job shredding all that cabbage. We also had lots of potatoes, about fifty bushels, to last through the winter. Everything was done by hand, so it was hard on the back. Strawberries were plentiful, so we always had jam to make all summer.

After all the work was done, we could go out and play baseball or tag in the evening. Washing was a big chore because we didn't have an electric washer, so we had to work it by hand and hang it all on the wash line. You can imagine how long it took to do all our clothes for twelve people.

I always liked to read. We could get books from the library to read when we had time. I liked spelling and arithmetic best, but I always got good grades. I did a lot of solos for weekday masses at church and was a good singer in those days.

None of us went to high school because of the transportation problem—buses were not in existence then, and my mother didn't drive. Maple Park was the closest school, so hardly anyone went to high school. I did housework for different people for around $2.50 a day, compared to ten dollars an hour today. We all did odd jobs after school to help with the budget because we weren't old enough to work and had no transportation. Katherine and Elizabeth were gone from home by then and stayed at homes where they worked.

When we were in school, we picked dandelions at noon hour for the pastor—about a few bushels that he would use to make dandelion wine with lots of sugar and raisins. It was fermented for about six weeks in a barrel. The longer it fermented, the stronger it got. Later on, it was used as vinegar. When we got all finished, the pastor always came out with hard candy for us—what a treat!

We didn't eat like the kids now days; potatoes and meat were our big thing. We never had store-bought bread. We had margarine but had to mix it to color it yellow and always use syrup instead of jelly. We had ice cream on the Fourth of July or a special occasion.

We had free movies on Friday night in the summer and maybe got a quarter to spend at the country store. The men went and had a few beers at the tavern while the women and the kids watched the movie. That was about the only recreation we had during the week. We only got to go to town on Saturday night, and then we had to take turns—only two of us could go out at one time.

Our eggs were traded at the country store for groceries, and we had plenty of milk from the cows. We butchered a cow for the winter and canned most of it. We also butchered a pig and some chickens. My mother and dad made sausage, which they smoked for an hour for six weeks. We could eat it like summer sausage or have it cooked. You can see why we didn't have much free time.

Dad liked to make home brew—it resembled beer— and he and a few friends played a card game called "66" one Friday a month.

The guys would go to the creek and catch turtles and clean them, and Mother would make a big kettle of turtle soup with lots of vegetables. I didn't like it too well, but that was all we had for supper.

I was seventeen and a half when I married your father, and we lived with his mother and dad on a farm in Virgil. Having to make breakfast for eight boys was a big chore, with stacks of pancakes and sausage to feed them all. Your father worked at the Western Dairy for forty years. The farmers all brought milk in cans, which was pasteurized and shipped out in big trucks. Your father was the engineer and kept everything in running order. He had to wear white overalls, so I had a lot of washing to do. It went out of business, and George got sent to the Modern Dairy in Elgin, where he worked until he retired.

I stayed home and raised six daughters, which kept me quite busy. We moved to a house in Virgil and stayed there until I sold it after your father passed away. We were married for forty-two years and lived in the same place in Virgil.

I went to work at Boynton Plastics in St. Charles six months before your father passed away. Thank goodness I had a job or I would have starved because I was not old enough to collect Social Security. I worked forty-six hours, and a half day on Saturday. I worked there for ten years and then moved in with Anita and her ex and little Sarah in Geneva for two years. I was very fortunate and moved with Linda and Jim in Batavia and stayed there a few years, and I kept on working in St. Charles.

A few years later, I met Gil Leadingham and chummed around with him for a year when we decided to get married and move to St. Charles. We stayed there until we bought a ranch house in North Aurora and lived there until he passed away.

I moved to Elgin and got married in 1991 to Walter Colsten, and we lived there for twelve years until he passed away in 2005. Then I was left alone again. I hated living by myself, and the girls decided I should find a better place to live. I moved to Asbury Towers on July 9, 2006, stayed there for six months, and then moved to Plum Landing on Lake Street in Aurora on February 2, 2007. I am satisfied living here and have a lot of good friends. I hope to spend the rest of my life here.

I am so thankful I have my five daughters and sons-in-law to call when I need them. May God bless all of them and my grandkids.

All my Love,
Mom

Note: Ruth originally typed this letter and sent copies to Mom and all the sisters. Attached to Mom's copy was a sticky note from Ruth. It reads:

Dearest Little Mother:

Roses are Red,

Violets are Blue,

Your writing is excellent,

And so are *you*!

Love, Ruth

December 6, 2008

Frances Mary Schmitt
Born March 16, 1920

This is a little write up of my life many years ago.

I was born in Aurora, Illinois. At the age of one, we moved to Maple Park and rented a farm because of my dad's health—he had emphysema.

My dad was born in Wheaton, a small family of one girl and three boys. My mother was born in Perham, Minnesota. There were three girls and one boy in her family. At the age of sixteen, Mom came to St. Charles and lived with her cousin. She later met my dad, and they got married in 1913. They had twelve children; I am the third oldest of the gang.

We all lived on a farm between Maple Park and Virgil. Most of us went as far as eighth grade. We didn't go to high school because of transportation problems. Buses weren't in existence then until later on when my younger brothers and sisters had a bus coming to pick them up. Everything we learned we got at grade school or by reading library books.

I graduated from grade school with fourteen kids, the biggest class in a long time, mostly because most kids stayed at home and worked with their family on the farms. Most of the farmers raised cattle and milked cows, and chickens for the eggs. The cattle were butchered for meat in the winter.

We didn't have much money, so we all worked on the farm or did housework for people who could afford to pay our high wages. We worked five or six hours a day for the big sum of $2.50 a day. We thought we were rich! We also had a couple of acres of land for a garden where we grew vegetables, melons, and squash. We spent a lot of time pulling weeds and harvesting vegetables.

Mom was always busy remodeling clothes and saving for us girls. Dad liked to cook and was always puttering in the kitchen. He loved to bake cakes and pies and candy at Christmas time.

Holidays were nothing like they are now. We had a raffle at the hall in Virgil on Thanksgiving, and they sold live turkeys. If my mother or dad were lucky, they would win a live turkey to bring home and butcher.

It was quite a messy job, but luckily Mom and Dad did it. Christmas was not like it is now either. We were lucky if we got a pair of gloves and a hat and maybe a small toy. But we were happy…

My two older sisters married first and left home. When I was seventeen and a half, I got married to George Altepeter, and we moved to a small house in Virgil. We had no electricity or indoor plumbing in the beginning and paid $1,400.00 for the house. George worked at Western Dairy in Virgil as a maintenance man until it closed down. He then worked at the Modern Dairy Milk Company until he retired. We lived in that little house for forty-two years until George passed away in 1979.

I lived in Virgil by myself for a year and then went to live with Anita, Jackie, and Sarah in Batavia. Later I moved in with Linda, Jim, Ben, Trina, and little Jacob until I was remarried in 1984 to Gilbert Leadingham. We lived in St. Charles in an apartment until we bought a house in North Aurora. We lived in North Aurora for eight years until Gil died from complications after surgery.

In 1993, I remarried Walter Colsten, and off I went to live in Elgin. I rented out the house in North Aurora. I was married to Walter for twelve years until he passed away.

I moved back to my house in North Aurora and lived there until I moved into Asbury Towers in North Aurora. Asbury closed suddenly after I was there only a year. Many of us were upset about it and made our feelings known to anybody who would listen. I became famous when I was interviewed by the newspapers and even ended up on the ten o'clock news.

This time I sold my house and moved to Plum Landing in Aurora on February 2, 2006. My best friend here is Doris Petrie, who lives two doors down from me. She helped me so much when I came home from the hospital.

I have a wonderful family of six girls. My oldest daughter died at seven weeks old. Helen came next and has three daughters and a son: Gretchen, Kelly, Vanessa, and Michelle. Helen also has nine grandchildren. Ruth and John have a boy and a girl and six grandchildren. Linda and Jim have two boys and a girl and two grandchildren.

Vicki and Larry have a girl and two boys and two grandchildren. Anita and Jim have two girls and two grandchildren. I can't attempt to mention all my grandchildren by name, but I love receiving pictures and letters from them and look forward to hearing from everyone. God bless you all.

I would like to wish everyone a Merry Christmas and a Happy New Year. With the economy the way it is, I will have to skip gifts this year, but please know that you are all in my heart and prayers always.

Love,
Grandma

Christmas 2009

Dear Family,

This will be a very short little note this year. The year has gone so fast, and my writing isn't too great.

I am still at Plum Landing, will be here three years in February. I am fairly well, have had some trouble with my breathing, but it's getting better. Nothing new going on around here. We lost people who left to go to homes closer to their families. We gained a few new ones, couples too. No new guys to interest me, though, so I just stick with my women friends.

Our place is all decorated for Christmas. We have lit up trees on every floor, so it is really colorful. We had our annual Christmas party on December 10. All the directors, their wives, and all the rest of us were there, so the place was packed. We all dressed up and had a very fancy dinner. We even had wine at our tables. They sure treat us well.

I don't get to see everyone because I don't like to go out when it's cold, snowy, or icy. Hope everyone is getting along well.

To all my family—daughters, sons-in-law, grandchildren, and great-grandchildren: You all make my life a joy, and I love you all so much.

Merry Christmas and Happy New Year.

All my love,
Grandma Fran

Grandma Fran's Letter

Loretta Marie Altepeter: 1938-1939

We are going back to November 6, 1937, when I married your father. We were married for a year when your sister Loretta Marie was born. It was a happy occasion for the both of us. She was born premature and only lived seven weeks. She had spina bifida and did not have a fully developed spine.

She weighed about six pounds but wasn't able to drink out of a bottle. It was a steady job trying to feed her with an eyedropper. She had to be fed every half hour. This went on for about seven weeks, but she kept on losing weight. Some of our friends came to stay the night. They helped take care of her in the night so I could get a little sleep. It was a painful experience.

She was born on November 11, 1938, and passed away on January 3, 1939. She had a little white casket, which we held on our laps while we took her to the cemetery. She was buried in the same grave as George's twin brother and sister were buried. They are all now in heaven waiting for us.

At times I think of her and your father, and I know they are in a safe place, praying for all of us. I am left with five daughters, who are my pride and joy, and a bunch of beautiful grandchildren to love.

God bless all of you,
Mom